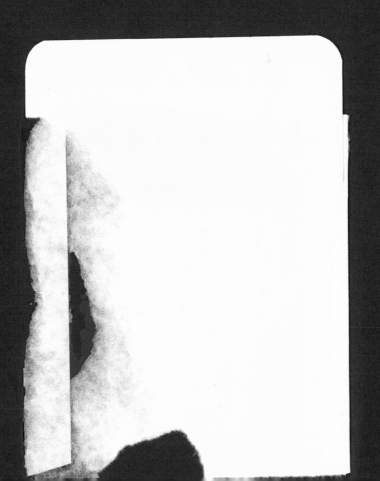

THE STRUGGLE FOR TENNESSEE
Tupelo to Stones River

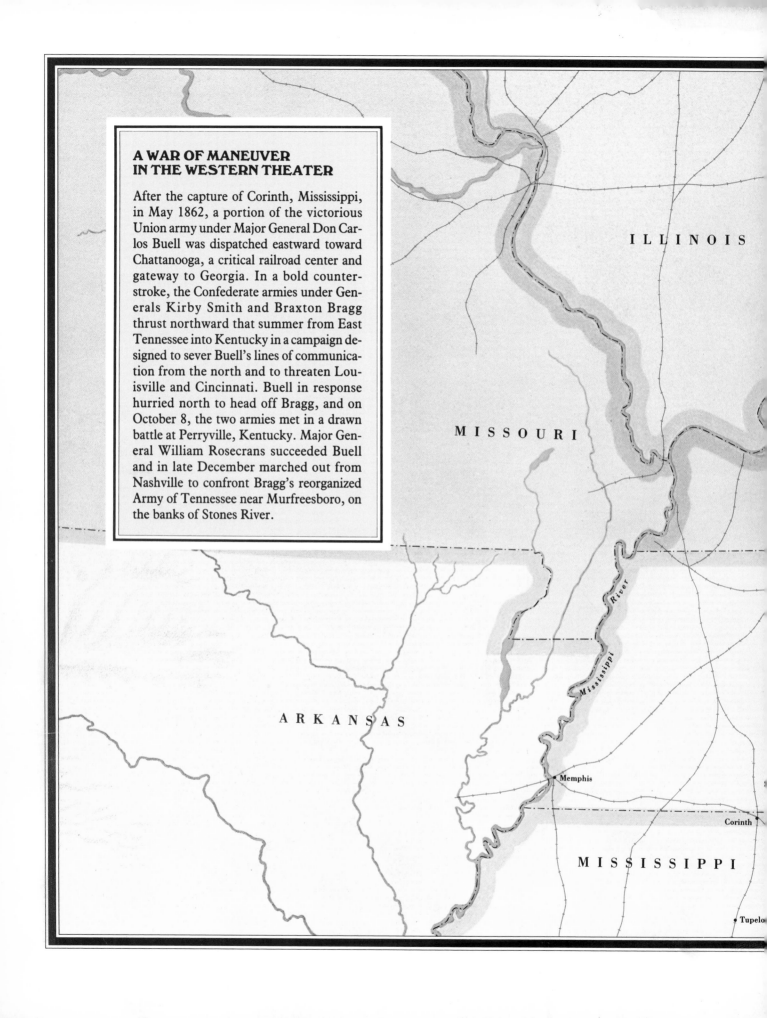

A WAR OF MANEUVER IN THE WESTERN THEATER

After the capture of Corinth, Mississippi, in May 1862, a portion of the victorious Union army under Major General Don Carlos Buell was dispatched eastward toward Chattanooga, a critical railroad center and gateway to Georgia. In a bold counterstroke, the Confederate armies under Generals Kirby Smith and Braxton Bragg thrust northward that summer from East Tennessee into Kentucky in a campaign designed to sever Buell's lines of communication from the north and to threaten Louisville and Cincinnati. Buell in response hurried north to head off Bragg, and on October 8, the two armies met in a drawn battle at Perryville, Kentucky. Major General William Rosecrans succeeded Buell and in late December marched out from Nashville to confront Bragg's reorganized Army of Tennessee near Murfreesboro, on the banks of Stones River.

ILLINOIS

MISSOURI

ARKANSAS

Mississippi River

Memphis

Corinth

MISSISSIPPI

Tupelo

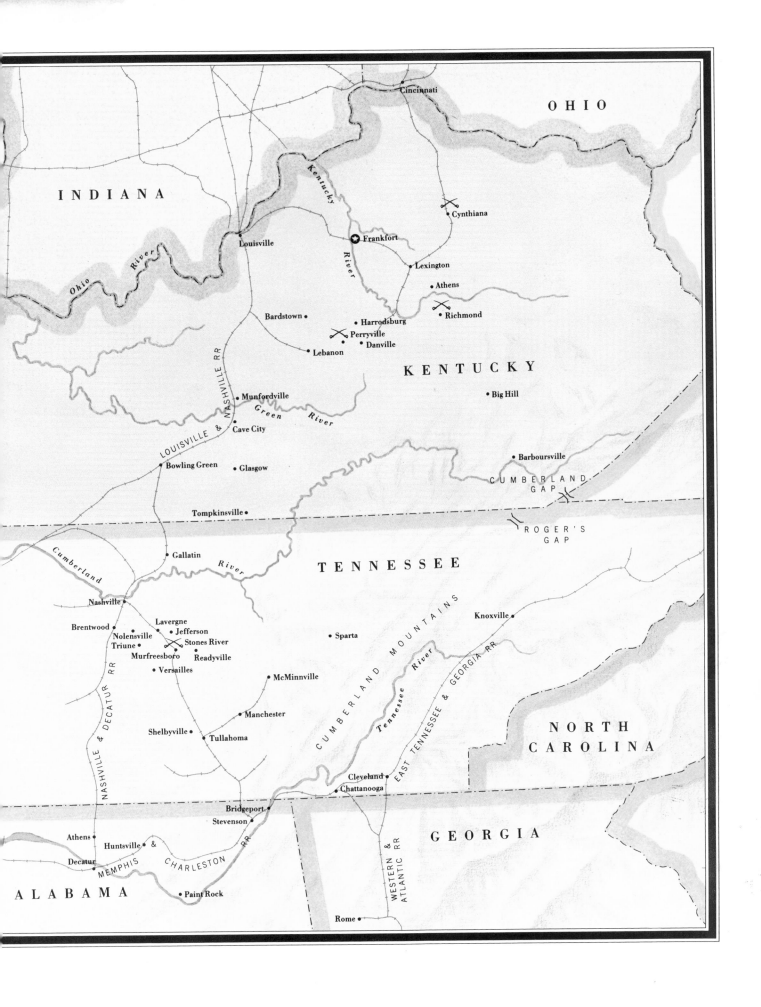

TIME® LIFE BOOKS

Other Publications:

UNDERSTANDING COMPUTERS
YOUR HOME
THE ENCHANTED WORLD
THE KODAK LIBRARY OF CREATIVE PHOTOGRAPHY
GREAT MEALS IN MINUTES
PLANET EARTH
COLLECTOR'S LIBRARY OF THE CIVIL WAR
THE EPIC OF FLIGHT
THE GOOD COOK
THE SEAFARERS
WORLD WAR II
HOME REPAIR AND IMPROVEMENT
THE OLD WEST

For information on and a full description of any of the
Time-Life Books series listed above, please write:
Reader Information, Time-Life Books
541 North Fairbanks Court, Chicago, Illinois 60611

This volume is one of a series that chronicles in full the
events of the American Civil War, 1861-1865.
Other books in the series include:
Brother against Brother: The War Begins
First Blood: Fort Sumter to Bull Run
The Blockade: Runners and Raiders
The Road to Shiloh: Early Battles in the West
Forward to Richmond: McClellan's Peninsular Campaign
Decoying the Yanks: Jackson's Valley Campaign
Confederate Ordeal: The Southern Home Front
Lee Takes Command: From Seven Days to Second Bull Run
The Coastal War: Chesapeake Bay to Rio Grande
Tenting Tonight: The Soldier's Life
The Bloodiest Day: The Battle of Antietam
War on the Mississippi: Grant's Vicksburg Campaign
Rebels Resurgent: Fredericksburg to Chancellorsville
Twenty Million Yankees: The Northern Home Front

The Cover: Federal troops supported by cannon
fire surge across Stones River in pursuit of retreating Confederates on January 2, 1863. The intense
fighting near Murfreesboro, Tennessee, cli-
maxed a Confederate campaign to drive the Union
army from Kentucky and central Tennessee, an effort that ended in frustration.

THE
CIVIL
WAR

THE STRUGGLE FOR TENNESSEE

BY

JAMES STREET JR.

AND THE

EDITORS OF TIME-LIFE BOOKS

Tupelo to Stones River

TIME-LIFE BOOKS, ALEXANDRIA, VIRGINIA

Time-Life Books Inc.
is a wholly owned subsidiary of
TIME INCORPORATED

FOUNDER: Henry R. Luce 1898-1967

Editor-in-Chief: Henry Anatole Grunwald
President: J. Richard Munro
Chairman of the Board: Ralph P. Davidson
Corporate Editor: Jason McManus
Group Vice President, Books: Reginald K. Brack Jr.
Vice President, Books: George Artandi

TIME-LIFE BOOKS INC.

EDITOR: George Constable
Executive Editor: George Daniels
Editorial General Manager: Neal Goff
Director of Design: Louis Klein
Editorial Board: Dale M. Brown, Roberta Conlan,
Ellen Phillips, Gerry Schremp, Donia Ann Steele,
Rosalind Stubenberg, Kit van Tulleken,
Henry Woodhead
Director of Research: Phyllis K. Wise
Director of Photography: John Conrad Weiser

PRESIDENT: William J. Henry
Senior Vice President: Christopher T. Linen
Vice Presidents: Stephen L. Bair, Robert A. Ellis,
John M. Fahey Jr., Juanita T. James, James L. Mercer,
Wilhelm R. Saake, Paul R. Stewart, Christian Strasser

The Civil War

Series Director: Henry Woodhead
Designer: Cynthia T. Richardson
Series Administrator: Philip Brandt George

Editorial Staff for *The Struggle for Tennessee*
Associate Editors: Thomas A. Lewis (text);
Jane Coughran (pictures)
Staff Writers: Thomas H. Flaherty Jr., R. W. Murphy,
David S. Thomson
Researchers: Harris J. Andrews, Sara Schneidman
(principals); Patti H. Cass, Brian C. Pohanka
Copy Coordinator: Kelly Banks
Picture Coordinator: Betty H. Weatherley
Editorial Assistant: Donna Fountain
Special Contributors: Karen G. Fitzwater, Brian McGinn

Editorial Operations
Design: Ellen Robling (assistant director)
Copy Chief: Diane Ullius
Editorial Operations: Caroline A. Boubin (manager)
Production: Celia Beattie
Quality Control: James J. Cox (director), Sally Collins
Library: Louise D. Forstall

Correspondents: Elisabeth Kraemer-Singh (Bonn);
Margot Hapgood, Dorothy Bacon (London); Miriam
Hsia (New York); Maria Vincenza Aloisi, Josephine du
Brusle (Paris); Ann Natanson (Rome). Valuable
assistance was also provided by: Lynne Bachleda
(Nashville); Carolyn Chubet (New York).

The Author:

James Street Jr. was born in Mississippi and had live[d]
every state of the old Confederacy by his 10th birth[day].
His great-grandfather served with Nathan Bedford F[or-]
rest during his later campaigns. A Ph.D. in history fr[om]
the University of North Carolina, Street has been a tea[ch-]
er, editor and publisher, and was a literary agent for [20?]
years. He is author of many articles and books, includ[ing]
Trout Flies and How to Tie Them and *James Street's So[uth]*.

The Consultants:

Colonel John R. Elting, USA (Ret.), a former Assoc[iate]
Professor at West Point, is the author of *Battles for Sca[ndi-]*
navia in the Time-Life Books World War II series an[d]
The Battle of Bunker's Hill, The Battles of Saratoga, M[ili-]
tary History and Atlas of the Napoleonic Wars and *Ameri[can]*
Army Life. Co-author of *A Dictionary of Soldier Talk*, h[e is]
also editor of the three volumes of *Military Uniform[s in]*
America, 1755-1867, and associate editor of *The West P[oint]*
Atlas of American Wars.

William A. Frassanito, a Civil War historian and lect[urer]
specializing in photograph analysis, is the author of [three]
award-winning studies, *Gettysburg: A Journey in Time[,]*
Antietam: The Photographic Legacy of America's Bloo[diest]
Day, and a companion volume, *Grant and Lee, The Vir[gin-]*
ia Campaigns. He has also served as chief consultant t[o the]
photographic history series *The Image of War*.

Les Jensen, Director of the Second Armored Divi[sion]
Museum, Fort Hood, Texas, specializes in Civil War [arti-]
facts and is a conservator of historic flags. He is a contri[bu-]
tor to *The Image of War* series, consultant for nume[rous]
Civil War publications and museums, and a membe[r of]
the Company of Military Historians. He was formerly [cu-]
rator of the U.S. Army Transportation Museum at [Fort]
Eustis, Virginia, and before that Curator of the Muse[um]
of the Confederacy in Richmond, Virginia.

Michael McAfee specializes in military uniforms and [has]
been Curator of Uniforms and History at the West P[oint]
Museum since 1970. A fellow of the Company of Mili[tary]
Historians, he coedited with Colonel Elting *Long End[ure:]*
The Civil War Years, and he collaborated with Frede[rick]
Todd on *American Military Equipage*. He is the autho[r of]
Artillery of the American Revolution, 1775-1783, and [has]
written numerous articles for *Military Images Magazi[ne]*.

James P. Shenton, Professor of History at Columbia [Uni-]
versity, is a specialist in 19th Century American polit[ical]
and social history, with particular emphasis on the C[ivil]
War period. He is the author of *Robert John Walker [and]*
Reconstruction South.

Library of Congress Cataloguing in Publication Data
Street, James, 1924-
   The struggle for Tennessee.
   (The Civil War)
   Bibliography: p.
   Includes index.
   1. Tennessee — History — Civil War, 1861-1865 —
Campaigns. 2. Kentucky — History — Civil War,
1861-1865 — Campaigns.   I. Time-Life Books.
II. Series.
E470.S77 1985   973.7'3013   85-8408
ISBN 0-8094-4760-6
ISBN 0-8094-4761-4 (lib. bdg.)

CONTENTS

Heyday for Raiders

"The great changes of command and commanders here has well nigh overburdened me, but I hope yet to mark the enemy before I break down."

GENERAL BRAXTON BRAGG, WRITING TO HIS WIFE FROM TUPELO, MISSISSIPPI, JULY 22, 1862

The mail train from Atlanta to Chattanooga rolled into Big Shanty, a whistlestop five miles north of Marietta, Georgia, and eased to a halt. In the misty, early-morning rain of Saturday, April 12, 1862, the crew and some of the passengers sauntered away to eat breakfast. The gleaming locomotive stood puffing quietly on the main line of the Western & Atlantic Railroad, its cab emblazoned with the name *General* in foot-high letters. The train seemed safe enough. Armed sentries were nearby, and the station was surrounded by the massed white tents of a Confederate army camp.

But 20 of the passengers did not go to breakfast. Instead, they disembarked and ambled toward the head of the train with a casual air that aroused no suspicion. Swiftly, four of the men uncoupled the *General*, its tender and three empty boxcars from the rest of the train and climbed aboard the locomotive, while the other men boarded the third boxcar.

The guards were unaware that anything was amiss until the *General* suddenly belched steam and, with connecting rods pounding and the big drive wheels spinning and shrieking on the rails, jerked the cars forward. Before the sentries could react, the train gathered speed and clattered away.

It did not take long for the astonished Confederates to realize that the train thieves were Federal irregulars bent on railroad sabotage — and operating within 25 miles of Atlanta. The raiders were, in fact, attached to a Federal army force advancing eastward through Tennessee with no less an objective than the capture of Chattanooga, one of the vital rail junctions of the Confederacy.

With the exception of their leader, a spy named James J. Andrews, and one other civilian volunteer, the audacious men were soldiers from Brigadier General Ormsby M. Mitchel's division of the Army of the Ohio. In February, that army, commanded by Major General Don Carlos Buell, had descended from Kentucky to occupy Nashville. In March, Mitchel's command of about 8,000 men had been detached to secure central Tennessee, while the rest of the army marched west under Buell to join General Ulysses S. Grant's advance on Corinth, Mississippi — by way of the killing ground around Shiloh Church.

Even though he was caught temporarily in a backwater of the War, Mitchel was not a man to idle away his time. The slender, wavy-haired West Pointer had left the Army in 1832 to teach mathematics and had made a name for himself writing and lecturing about astronomy. Commissioned a brigadier general at the outbreak of the War, he had proved to be a temperamental officer given to self-promotion. In too many communications sent to too many people, he tended to overemphasize his burdens and his achievements.

General Buell, who would be involved in bitter arguments with Mitchel, and about him, for years, never did figure out quite

eneral Braxton Bragg, an iron-handed disciplinarian, took over the battered Confederate army in Mississippi in June 1862 with orders to strike into Tennessee.

what to make of his subordinate. "In spite of his peculiarities," Buell wrote after the War, "General Mitchel was a valuable officer. He was not insubordinate, but was restless in ordinary service and ambitious in an ostentatious way."

Once his forces of occupation had taken a firm grip on central Tennessee, Mitchel found himself with time on his hands and a great deal of discretion. He discovered that as long as he sent reports to General Buell, he was free to take any action. It was not long before Mitchel had hatched a bold plot to capture Chattanooga in East Tennessee, 113 miles southeast of Nashville and just above the Georgia line.

Mountainous East Tennessee was a hotbed of pro-Union sentiment. President Abraham Lincoln had expressed intense interest in freeing Union sympathizers there from Confederate domination. More important still, Mitchel understood fully that the war west of the Appalachians was being fought as much for the railroads as for territory and that Chattanooga was vital to control of the rails.

Whoever possessed the railroads in the west held a key to the struggle being waged east of the Appalachians. To sustain its campaign north of Richmond, the Confederate Army of Northern Virginia was dependent on a constant flow of food, munitions, manufactures and manpower from the south and west. Two of the major arteries of that flow — the Western & Atlantic Railroad from Atlanta and the Memphis & Charleston from the Mississippi River at Memphis and points west — met just east of Chattanooga, at Cleveland, Tennessee; there the two combined to form the East Tennessee & Georgia Railroad, which wound northeastward

through the Allegheny Mountains to Virginia. "To take and hold the railroad at or east of Cleveland," President Lincoln would say, "I think fully as important as the taking and holding of Richmond."

Mitchel was gambling that the Federal armies to his west would have little trouble occupying their first objective on the Memphis & Charleston Railroad — Corinth, Mississippi, just south of Shiloh — and that they would then turn eastward toward Chattanooga. And so in April of 1862, he set out on his self-appointed mission to lead the way to Chattanooga — and garner the glory.

Thus began a vicious, sprawling struggle between opposing armies that for the next eight months would seesaw through eastern Tennessee and Kentucky, spilling over at times into Alabama and Georgia. The Federal advance toward Chattanooga would be countered by Confederate incursions north toward Lexington and Louisville. And just as the proximity of Mitchel's Federal raiders had alarmed Atlanta in April, so in September the approach of a Confederate army would terrify the citizens of Cincinnati, Ohio, more than 350 miles to the north. In October, the enemy armies would collide in battle near Perryville, Kentucky. And the end of the year would find them back in Tennessee, locked in bloody combat on the banks of Stones River.

On April 8, the day after the Federals won the field at Shiloh, General Mitchel moved from his base near Nashville south to seize Huntsville, Alabama, a town on the Memphis & Charleston line. From there he intended to push eastward and, if all went well, to take lightly defended Chattanooga and hold it until the main army arrived. The spy

The wood-burning locomotive *General* is displayed at a reunion of Federal veterans in Columbus, Ohio after the War. Volunteers from three Ohio regiments served in the raiding party that stole the *General* from under the noses of the Confederates in April 1862.

Andrews and his raiders had already been dispatched on a mission to destroy bridges and track along the Western & Atlantic so that reinforcements could not be rushed to Chattanooga from the south.

On April 11, the day before Andrews and his men roared out of Big Shanty with the stolen train, Mitchel took Huntsville completely by surprise, seizing 200 prisoners, 15 locomotives and a large number of cars. Then Mitchel used his captured rolling stock to occupy key positions along 70 miles of the railroad in both directions, west to Decatur and east to Stevenson, just 35 miles from Chattanooga. Never one to understate his accomplishments, Mitchel reported to Buell's headquarters, "We have at length succeeded in cutting the great artery of railroad intercommunication between the Southern States."

Thus far, Mitchel had performed aggressively and well — and for his efforts was promoted to Major General. But then things began to go disastrously wrong, especially for Andrews' raiders. In their flight northward from Big Shanty, the raiders had been pursued so hotly that there had been no time to tear up track or burn bridges. Finally, 18 miles south of Chattanooga, they ran out of fuel, abandoned the locomotive and ran for their lives. All of them were captured. Andrews and seven others were hanged as spies;

eight of the men later escaped and made their way back to Federal territory; and the rest were eventually exchanged.

Although he was only a few days' march from Chattanooga, Mitchel did not dare advance as long as the Western & Atlantic line remained open to enemy traffic. His pleas to Buell for reinforcements were ignored; Buell's troops and other Federal forces under Major General Henry W. Halleck, now overall commander in the west, had been committed to an advance southward from the Shiloh battlefield to the railroad town of Corinth. This glacial passage of 15 miles began at the end of April and consumed the entire month of May; by the time the Federals arrived, the outnumbered Confederates had abandoned Corinth and retreated 50 miles south to Tupelo, Mississippi.

As he waited for reinforcements, Mitchel had his hands full trying to maintain his hold on the stretch of railroad he had seized. There were few Confederate troops in northern Alabama, but the thinly spread Federals were continually attacked by bands of guerrillas, who were supported and concealed by sympathetic residents of the countryside.

Mitchel's men reacted harshly to the assaults by the elusive irregulars. While Colonel John Beatty of the 3rd Ohio Infantry was moving his regiment to Huntsville during May, his train was ambushed near the town of Paint Rock, and several of his men were wounded. "I had the train stopped," Beatty wrote in his diary, "and, taking a file of soldiers, returned to the village. The telegraph line had been cut, and the wire was lying in the street. Calling the citizens together, I said to them that this bushwhacking must cease. Hereafter every time the telegraph wire was cut we would burn a house; every

Protected by a detachment of infantry *(left)*, men of the 1st Michigan Engineers and Mechanics labor in the July heat to repair a railroad bridge across the Elk River in southern Tennessee. The bridge, which had been burned by the Confederates, was part of the tenuous life line between the Federal army at Decatur, Alabama, and its supply base in Nashville, about 100 miles to the north.

time a train was fired upon we should hang a man; and we would continue to do this until every house was burned and every man was hanged between Decatur and Bridgeport. I then set fire to the town, took three citizens with me, and proceeded to Huntsville."

Drastic as it was, Beatty's reaction was no less violent than that of another of Mitchel's officers, Colonel John Basil Turchin. In reprisal for a guerrilla attack on men of his 19th Illinois in Athens, Alabama, the Russian-born Turchin turned the town over to the regiment, declaring, "I shut mine eyes for one hour." In that time the vengeful troops stripped the residents of watches, jewelry and silver, and raped a number of slave girls. The citizens of Athens later filed 45 affidavits claiming that Turchin's men had stolen more than $50,000 worth of goods.

Despite the harassment by partisans, Mitchel tried to extend his occupation of the railroad—with mixed results. On April 17 a brigade commanded by Colonel Turchin headed east from Decatur and, without opposition, advanced 40 more miles down the railroad toward Chattanooga. But on hearing a rumor that Confederate forces were threatening from the direction of Corinth, Mitchel ordered his men back to Decatur, and there he had them burn behind them the railroad bridge over the Tennessee River.

Then, 12 days later, Mitchel led an expedition eastward beyond Stevenson and drove a small Confederate force away from Bridgeport; there he captured the railroad bridge over the Tennessee and burned a smaller bridge beyond the town. Then Mitchel proceeded to advertise his achievements. He had already begun sending reports directly to Secretary of War Edwin M. Stanton, and on May 1 he had stirring news for Washing-

ton: "This campaign is now ended, and I can now occupy Huntsville in perfect security, while all of Alabama north of the Tennessee floats no flag but that of the Union." Stanton was pleased, and he was not alone in his approval. The Secretary sent word to Mitchel that his "spirited operations afford great satisfaction to the President."

Doubtless Mitchel's lively reports pro-

Major General Don Carlos Buell, a West Point-trained career officer, was a stickler for discipline and detail, with an ultracautious approach to combat. Buell had little confidence in the volunteers who made up his Federal Army of the Ohio — and his men had little love for him.

vided a refreshing contrast to news of Halleck's plodding march from Shiloh to Corinth. Yet trouble lay in store for the boastful Mitchel. When the movement to Corinth finally concluded, Halleck, as expected, dispatched General Buell and his troops eastward to take Chattanooga. And Buell would be much less satisfied than Stanton or Lincoln with the accomplishments of his subordinate.

Despite a violent temper that repeatedly got him into trouble, Major General Don Carlos Buell had performed brilliantly at West Point. In the Mexican War, where he was wounded, he served with distinction, receiving three brevet promotions. Thereafter he had transferred from the 3rd United States Infantry to the adjutant general's department, perhaps in search of rapid promotion, and had worked there creditably for 13 years, rising to the rank of lieutenant colonel. After the War started and General George B. McClellan, the Federal General in Chief, chose him to lead the Army of the Ohio, Buell proved to be a cautious, methodical soldier. He was an excellent disciplinarian and a hard worker, but he was also rigid, opinionated and unpopular. Colonel Beatty described him as "cold, smooth-toned, silent."

General Halleck had high hopes for Buell's eastward push. A rapid march would claim East Tennessee and its railroad network, prevent the Confederates at Tupelo and Chattanooga from combining their forces — and even more, as Halleck intimated. On June 12, Halleck informed Stanton that Buell would reach Decatur on June 13. Then Halleck added, much to his later embarrassment, "If the enemy should have evacuated East Tennessee and Cumberland Gap, as reported, Buell will probably move on to Atlanta."

But Buell's march bogged down at Decatur — and he placed some of the blame on Ormsby Mitchel. Buell complained about being slowed down by having to repair the railroad, especially the bridge that Mitchel had ordered burned.

The destroyed bridge prevented Buell from easily supplying his 31,000 troops on the march, but that was not the only impediment. Confederate guerrillas had wrecked rails and damaged rolling stock. Ordinarily the Tennessee River would have served as an avenue of supply, but hot, dry weather had so depleted the waterway and its tributaries that boats could not reach Buell's troops.

Nor was Buell's staff up to the logistical task. On June 27, when he arrived in Athens, Alabama, just north of Decatur, he thought his worst problems would soon be over. He had ordered that a five-day supply of rations for his men be shipped to Athens from the Federal base at Nashville. But the complicated staff work required to execute the orders had been completely botched. The army was placed on half rations, and a week later Buell complained, "We are living from day to day on short supplies and our operations are completely crippled."

Another commander might simply have taken what he needed from the countryside. But Buell believed in traditional warfare, which isolated civilians from harm as much as possible. Treating the locals mildly might win their favor, he thought, and he forbade looting the countryside even in reprisal for bushwhacking. Over this issue, Buell was to heap wrath on the shoulders of his subordinate, General Mitchel.

After the supply debacle at Athens, Buell joined Mitchel at Huntsville and was even more outraged at what he found there. Buell later fumed that Mitchel failed to repair the railroad and assemble supplies for the army as ordered; further, Buell leveled the charge that Mitchel had allowed his troops to run wild, that "imperfect discipline and an injudicious temper on the part of the commander of the troops had embittered even that portion of the population that would have been friendly or passive."

Mitchel had made a feeble attempt to deal with the discipline problem. He had complained to the Secretary of War that "the most terrible outrages — robberies, rapes, arsons and plunderings — are being committed by lawless brigands and vagabonds connected with the army." Mitchel had even re-

ceived the authority to sentence offenders to death, but he never used it.

Buell found on his arrival in Huntsville that no offender had been punished; he also learned that such incidents were not isolated, that indeed, "not only straggling individuals, but a whole brigade, under the open authority of its commander, could engage in these acts." He was referring to the earlier sacking of Athens by Colonel Turchin.

Buell acted with resolution. He had Turchin court-martialed and dismissed from the service. But Buell won few friends among superiors or subordinates. Colonel Beatty, whose burning of Paint Rock had apparently escaped censure, sat on Turchin's court-martial. Beatty wrote in his diary that in dealing with the Confederate irregulars, "Turchin has gone to one extreme, but Buell

is inaugurating the dancing-master policy: 'By your leave, my dear sir, we will have a fight; that is, if you are sufficiently fortified; no hurry; take your own time.' To the bushwhacker: 'Am sorry you gentlemen fire at our trains from behind stumps, logs and ditches. Had you not better cease this sort of warfare?' " Buell's policy, Beatty lamented, was "that of an amiable idiot."

Abraham Lincoln apparently was none too pleased, either. After hearing a plea from Turchin's wife, the President not only reinstated Turchin but promoted him to brigadier general. Mitchel was served less well by events: When he angrily demanded a transfer to escape Buell's authority, he was given command of the Department of the South, the Federal foothold on the coasts of Georgia, South Carolina and Florida. There he contracted yellow fever and died on October 30, 1862.

Despite his unpopularity, Buell managed to prevail. When in mid-July General Halleck was summoned to Washington to take command of all Union forces, the Department of the West was split into several commands. General Ulysses S. Grant, with the largest force, about 67,000 men, was to guard rail communications and occupy towns in Union-held territory in the west, but he would concentrate on taking Vicksburg, the last principal Confederate bastion on the Mississippi River. Buell, meanwhile, continued in command of the Department of the Ohio and pressed on with the job of taking Chattanooga and clearing East Ten-

nessee. But before Buell could resume the march eastward, Confederate surprise attacks thwarted his plans yet again.

The principal Confederate forces that posed a threat to Buell in East Tennessee were the 56,000-man Army of the Mississippi, which had been pulling itself together at Tupelo after its retreat from Corinth, and the 10,000 men under Major General Edmund Kirby Smith, who were based in Chattanooga.

With the death at Shiloh of General Albert Sidney Johnston, command of the Army of the Mississippi had passed to another full general of glittering reputation, Pierre Gustave Toutant Beauregard of Louisiana. But Beauregard, acclaimed as the hero of Fort Sumter and Bull Run, had clashed repeatedly with President Jefferson Davis and had served without distinction during the Confederate defeats at Fort Henry, Fort Donelson and Shiloh. After Beauregard abandoned strategic Corinth without a fight, Davis replaced him in June with General Braxton Bragg.

Bragg, at 46, shared a remarkable number of traits with the man who was to become his principal antagonist, General Buell. Bragg, like Buell, had shown great early promise, graduating fifth in the West Point class of 1837 and later serving with distinction as an artillery officer in the War with Mexico, where he garnered three brevets.

But Bragg was prey to frequent disabling illnesses, from dyspepsia to headaches. Perhaps because of these illnesses, he was ex-

The Tennessee River flows placidly through heavily wooded country near Knoxville in this 1861 painting by the noted Southern landscape artist James Ca▸

rn Tennessee's mountains and primeval forests made that region ideal for guerrilla operations and difficult territory for any army to control.

ceedingly unpleasant to everyone around him. General Grant, who served with him in Mexico, remembered Bragg as "a remarkably intelligent and well-informed man," who was "thoroughly upright. But he was possessed of an irascible temper and was naturally disputatious. As a subordinate he was always on the lookout to catch his commanding officer infringing upon his prerogatives; as a post commander he was equally vigilant to detect the slightest neglect, even of the most trivial order."

Bragg married the daughter of a wealthy Louisiana planter, then he left the Army in 1856 to purchase and operate his own sugar plantation. He prospered and soon became influential in Louisiana affairs. Early in the War he was commissioned a brigadier general by his friend and fellow West Pointer, Jefferson Davis. It was not long, however, before the flaws in Bragg's character and the sourness of his personality had become obvious to all.

Bragg's touchstone was discipline. During the fighting at Shiloh he had repeatedly ordered costly, unavailing charges; after the battle he blamed the Confederate defeat on "want of discipline and a want of officers. Universal suffrage, furloughs and whiskey have ruined us."

At Corinth, when a Tennessee regiment found its one-year term of enlistment extended by the Confederate conscription act, the men agreed to continue in service but insisted on a brief leave to visit their homes. Bragg held the soldiers in their place by deploying a battery of artillery and threatening to open fire on them.

Not surprisingly, then, Bragg's first order of business on replacing Beauregard at Tupelo was to whip his army into shape—literally. To be sure, the need for improvement was urgent. Bragg knew he could do little against the superior Federal forces to the north until his army—"the mob we have miscalled soldiers," as he condescendingly put it—was better trained, in good health and of sound morale.

But his rigorous discipline and training were imposed with a brutality that appalled his soldiers. Private Sam Watkins of the 1st Tennessee wrote that Bragg was looked upon as a merciless tyrant. "He loved to crush the spirit of his men," said Watkins. "The more of a hangdog look they had about them the better was General Bragg pleased. Not a single soldier in the whole army ever loved or respected him."

Watkins cited the punishment of a man who had been absent without leave for 10 days; the offending soldier was forced to kneel, his head was shaved "slick as a peeled onion" and he was stripped. "Then a strapping fellow with a big rawhide would make the blood flow and spurt at every lick, the wretch begging and howling like a hound, and then he was branded with a red hot iron with the letter D on both hips."

For all its cruelty, such treatment must have had the desired effect; another soldier wrote in July of 1862 that "there has been a marvelous change for the better in the condition, discipline and drill of the troops." Bragg himself was pleased, writing his wife that the army had shown a marked improvement, "so that we are now in a high state of efficiency, health and tone. We shall be on the move very soon."

But first, of course, Bragg had to decide where to go. Like Beauregard before him, Bragg was under general instructions from the War Department in Richmond to strike northward, through Buell's strung-out Federal army, to Nashville. But decisive action had never been easy for Bragg, and from the beginning his deliberations on how to accomplish this objective had been complicated by Major General Edmund Kirby Smith over at Chattanooga.

Early in the spring, Kirby Smith had been given the daunting responsibility of holding the East Tennessee & Georgia Railroad between Chattanooga and the Cumberland Gap — a distance of 180 miles — with only six small brigades. The task had driven Smith to distraction.

In addition to the pressure from Mitchel, Smith had had to deal with two other independent commands left by General Buell in central Tennessee. First, Federal Brigadier General George W. Morgan had threatened from the north, advancing into Cumberland Gap with 9,000 troops. Then a 6,000-man force under Brigadier General James S. Negley had approached Chattanooga from the northwest, on June 7 actually shelling the city as if in preparation for an assault. Now Buell was advancing, however slowly, with his Army of the Ohio reinforced to a strength of 55,000. Smith pleaded with Bragg and with his superiors in Richmond for more troops, arguing that his men were worn out from the constant shuttling back and forth between threatened spots. Technically, Smith's was an independent command, but President Jefferson Davis encouraged Bragg to cooperate with Smith if possible.

Smith was nursing invasion plans of his own. Despite the growing threat to Chattanooga, he wanted to strike into Kentucky. He believed there were thousands of Confederate sympathizers there, chafing under the Federal yoke and ready to take up arms to help him occupy the state. In early July he unleashed two preliminary raids led by relatively inexperienced cavalry commanders. These raids would have a calamitous effect, both on Buell's just-resumed advance toward Chattanooga and on Bragg's half-formed plans to strike toward Nashville.

One of Smith's cavalry commanders was Colonel John Hunt Morgan, a wealthy businessman from Lexington who possessed all of the attributes commonly associated with a Kentucky gentleman; he was tall and handsome, with refined manners and an easygoing style. While he savored the dash and glamor of raiding, Morgan was neither reckless nor flamboyant; but he did attract flamboyant subordinates.

Among them was George St. Leger Grenfell, a British soldier of fortune who rode into camp with a red-tasseled turban on his head and two hunting dogs trotting at his horse's heels. To hear him tell it, Grenfell had served with the French in Algeria, had charged with the Light Brigade in the Crimea, and had fought against the Sepoy Rebellion in India and with Garibaldi in South America. Though he may have exaggerated his exploits, Grenfell carried a letter from Robert E. Lee recommending him for any position. Morgan, who liked Grenfell immediately, made the Briton his adjutant.

Also on Morgan's staff were talents such as George (Lightning) Ellsworth, an expert telegrapher, wiretap artist and comedian, and Basil W. Duke, Morgan's second-in-command and brother-in-law. The staff and most of the brigade's 900 men affected the trappings of cavaliers — broad-brimmed hats, high boots, enormous spurs and flowing beards. On July 4 they trotted out of

Knoxville bent on harassing the vital Federal supply line between Nashville and Louisville, Kentucky.

Plagued by pro-Union bushwhackers who abounded in East Tennessee mountains, the raiders nevertheless were able to make the 104-mile westward ride across the Cumberland Plateau to Sparta, Tennessee, in three days. There, as Smith and Morgan had expected, the people were sympathetic to the Confederate cause; new recruits flocked to join the raiders.

Among the volunteers was a guerrilla named Champ Ferguson, who had earned a reputation for barbaric treatment of prisoners. One of Morgan's men wrote of Ferguson: "Ill-treatment of his wife and daughter by some soldiers and Home-guards enlisted in his own neighborhood made him relentless in his hatred of all Union men. He had a brother of the same character as himself in the Union army, and they sought each other persistently, mutually bent on fratricide. The mountains of Kentucky and Tennessee were filled with such men, who murdered every prisoner they took."

Morgan left Sparta with his brigade, now numbering 1,100 men, to attack a Federal garrison at Tompkinsville, Kentucky, 90 miles to the northeast. Doubtless he relished the idea of taking Tompkinsville, for he knew that the town was defended by a battalion of the 9th Pennsylvania Cavalry commanded by Major Thomas Jefferson Jordan. Back in May, those same Pennsylvanians had occupied the Kentucky village of Lebanon and had insulted the women there by using vulgar language and advising them that the only way to preserve their virtue was, as Jordan put it, "to sew up the bottoms of their petticoats."

The Flair of a Cavalryman

From his silver spurs to his hand-tooled Mexican saddle, John Hunt Morgan projected the image of a dashing Southern cavalier. The portrait below shows Morgan in the informal garb he wore while campaigning; for formal occasions, he donned a general's gilt-braided kepi and frock coat, shown at right. Morgan's bone-handled Colt .44 revolvers were a matched pair, and his ornate saddle, a masterpiece of craftsmanship, was an 1862 gift from grateful admirers in Augusta, Georgia.

Colonel George St. Leger Grenfell
an English soldier of fortune, becan
John Hunt Morgan's adjutant and
took on the impossible task of teac
ing Morgan's free-wheeling
Confederate horsemen the basics
military discipline and drill.

Morgan's brother-in-law, Colonel
Basil W. Duke, a Kentucky lawyer,
became Morgan's second-in-comm
at the age of 24. At 26, Duke was
commanding a Confederate cavalry
brigade of his own.

Morgan's brigade reached Tompkinsville on July 9 and quickly surrounded the 400 Federal troops, who were deployed on a thickly wooded hill. After a brief flurry of musketry, Major Jordan surrendered. All the Federal prisoners except Jordan were paroled; presumably for his offense against Southern womanhood, Jordan was sent to prison in Richmond.

When Morgan's force reached the Louisville & Nashville telegraph line, 30 miles north of Tompkinsville, Ellsworth tapped the wire and began spreading the false information that Morgan intended to strike all the way to the Ohio River and attack Louisville and Cincinnati. The bogus reports were widely believed; alarms were raised throughout the Ohio River valley, and panic spread through Cincinnati and Louisville. To fuel the fear, Morgan marched to the banks of the Ohio northeast of Louisville.

Sweeping eastward, Morgan on July 17 approached Cynthiana, a town on the Licking River south of Cincinnati. Cynthiana and its Kentucky Central Railroad depot were defended by an unsuspecting Federal contingent under the command of Colonel John J. Landrum. Landrum had only one cannon, a brass 12-pounder, and all but a handful of his 340 men were either green recruits or ill-trained Home Guards.

Morgan announced his presence by ordering Captain Joseph E. Harris' horse artillery to open fire on the town. Then he launched a three-pronged assault. Lieutenant Colonel Basil Duke's 2nd Kentucky Cavalry attacked across the river from the west while Major Richard Gano's battalion of Texans and Tennesseans, who had crossed to the rear of the town, charged down the main street. A third force, Captain F. M. Nix's 1st

Georgia, charged on Duke's left.

Colonel Landrum set up his lone cannon in the town square and tried desperately to organize a defense. But Confederate crossfire soon forced the crew to abandon the weapon.

Landrum and some of his men took shelter in the railroad depot. But Harris' gunners had pushed their fieldpieces across the bridge by hand and turned them on the depot at point-blank range. The Federal resistance collapsed. Landrum told his surviving troops to "save yourselves, and I will do likewise." Landrum and a few men escaped, but Morgan took the rest prisoner, along with a much-needed herd of 300 horses.

The skirmish at Cynthiana served Morgan's larger purpose well. Federal Brigadier General Jeremiah T. Boyle, commanding in Louisville, fired off requests for reinforcements in all directions: to Governor Oliver Morton in Indiana, to General Buell in Alabama and directly to Washington.

Morton sent a few raw recruits. Buell wired back that he could spare no troops because he was expecting an attack on his own lines. Lincoln responded by wiring Halleck at Corinth: "They are having a stampede in Kentucky. Please look to it." Halleck then

Champ Ferguson, a Kentucky woodsman turned guerrilla, joined Morgan's cavalry as a guide after promising to give up his practice of killing Yankee prisoners.

wired Buell: "Do all in your power to put down the Morgan raid even if the Chattanooga expedition should be delayed."

But by that time Morgan and his raiders were already on their way back to Tennessee. In just over three weeks they had ridden 1,000 miles, had taken 1,200 prisoners, captured 17 towns and destroyed or turned over to local sympathizers a small fortune in Federal property. More important, the raid had distracted Federal attention from the advance on Chattanooga.

Although no more than about 300 volunteers had actually joined the raiders in Kentucky, Morgan persisted in his belief that Bluegrass men were anxious to sign up with the Confederate forces. At one point he telegraphed Kirby Smith to assure him that if the general's army were to advance into Kentucky, "25,000 or 30,000 men will join you at once."

In fact, the recruiters who benefited most from Morgan's raid were Federal. More than 7,000 pro-Union men were worried enough about the Confederate raiders to enlist in seven Kentucky cavalry regiments. Volunteers also rushed to the colors in Indiana. And in Ohio, a recruiting officer — Colonel Rutherford B. Hayes, a future President of the

United States — was so gratified by the flood of volunteers that he was moved to cheer "Hooray for Morgan!"

On July 6, two days after Morgan had left Knoxville, another of Kirby Smith's cavalry commanders, Colonel Nathan Bedford Forrest, had left Chattanooga with 1,000 troopers. Forrest's mission was the same as Morgan's — to disrupt the tenuous Federal supply line extending from Louisville to Buell's army. His chief target was Murfreesboro, an important depot on the Nashville & Chattanooga Railroad.

Forrest, like Morgan, had been a wealthy businessman before the War and behaved as if born to the saddle and to command. But Forrest had emerged from a background of poverty with the benefit of only six months of formal schooling, and he was as rough-hewn as Morgan was polished. A former planter and slave trader, Forrest was quick with his fists and a tenacious leader who loathed giving ground no matter how desperate the circumstances. When his cavalry was among the Confederate forces surrounded at Fort Donelson, he had been disgusted at his superiors' surrender and had led his troops out in a daring escape. At Shiloh, Forrest had covered the Confederate retreat with a slashing rearguard action in which he had been seriously wounded.

Despite his achievements and his popularity among most of his troops, Forrest was scorned by many West Pointers for his nonprofessional background. And throughout the War, the unlettered Mississippian remained socially unacceptable to the aristocratic Southerners who made up a good part of the Confederate cavalry officer corps. "I must express my distaste," a fellow Missis-

John Hunt Morgan posted this broadside and others like it as he rode through Kentucky in July 1862, urging the citizens of his native state to rise against "the hireling legions of Lincoln." Morgan's raid attracted some Kentuckians to the Confederate cause, but it frightened many others into enlisting in Union regiments.

sippian would write later, "to being commanded by a man having no pretension to gentility, an ambitious man careless of the lives of his men. I object to a tyrannical, hotheaded vulgarian's commanding me." Despite such complaints, however, Forrest, in July of 1862, was about to be promoted to brigadier general.

Late on the night of July 12, Forrest halted his column in Woodbury, Tennessee, 18 miles east of Murfreesboro. By now his brigade had swelled to 1,400 men, most of them belonging to two regiments: Colonel John A. Wharton's 8th Texas Cavalry and the 2nd Georgia Cavalry under Colonel William J. Lawton. Various additional companies and battalions of Georgia, Tennessee and Kentucky troopers not assigned to regiments had joined Forrest en route. The men had never before fought together as a brigade, but they had followed Forrest willingly across 100 miles of rugged mountain terrain in six days.

The people of Woodbury were overjoyed to see Forrest's troopers. The townspeople related that only the previous evening, Federal cavalry had swept into the town, arrested nearly all of the male residents, charged them with being Confederate sympathizers and spies, and taken them to jail in Murfreesboro. The townsfolk claimed that six of the prisoners were to be hanged in Murfreesboro the following morning.

With no hesitation, Forrest promised the townspeople he would prevent the executions. "This had a happy effect," a colonel on Forrest's staff wrote later. "All vied with each other in a liberal hospitality, and an abundance of food and forage was provided for the command."

Murfreesboro was defended by a full brigade of Federal troops, but they were widely scattered and inefficiently led. On July 11, a new commander, Brigadier General Thomas T. Crittenden, had taken charge of the 1,400-man garrison. Crittenden had realized immediately that his defenses would have to be improved; but as there had not been a Confederate force closer than Chattanooga since February, he decided that he had plenty of time.

He was wrong. Before dawn on July 13, Forrest sent Colonel Wharton and a detachment of his 8th Texas Cavalry on a reconnaissance toward Murfreesboro. They returned an hour later with 15 captured Federal pickets, who admitted that the Murfreesboro garrison had no inkling of Forrest's presence. The prisoners also disclosed that the Federals had one camp just west of town and another even farther west on the bank of Stones River.

Forrest issued orders for an attack at first light. Wharton would engage the Federals encamped on the outskirts of town. Meanwhile, part of the 2nd Georgia under Lieutenant Colonel Arthur Hood would dash into the center of town to seize the jail and free the men from Woodbury. Lieutenant Colonel James T. Morrison would join the charge with the remainder of the 2nd Georgia and part of the 8th Texas to take the courthouse and other key buildings, including General Crittenden's headquarters at the hotel. Another column commanded by Colonel Lawton was to circle the town to the west to cut off any advance from the Federal encampment on the river.

With first light, Wharton's cavalrymen charged into the Federal camp near town, taking a detail of the 7th Pennsylvania Cavalry completely by surprise and stampeding the dismounted troopers into the nearby tents of Colonel William W. Duffield's 9th Michigan Infantry. Despite the confusion, Duffield was able to form a line of battle, steady his men and open fire. Now it was the Texans' turn to be driven back. In the exchange of fire, both Wharton and Duffield went down with serious wounds.

Duffield's replacement, Lieutenant Colonel John G. Parkhurst, feared that his Federals could not withstand a second assault in

Near the end of his 24-day raid, John Hunt Morgan — on a prancing horse (*right foreground*) — and his Confederate cavalry pause in the town square at Paris, the county seat of Bourbon County in northern Kentucky. By this time, three Union forces were pursuing Morgan, but he outrode them back to Tennessee.

General Nathan Bedford Forrest was usually outnumbered in battle, but he excelled at concentrating his Confederate cavalry at a single point of attack and would then lead the charge himself with reckless courage. His simple maxim was "to get there first with the most men."

their present position. He ordered a hasty retreat to the cover of a nearby wooden fence. The men added further protection by overturning supply wagons behind the fence. The wagons were barely in place when Confederate Lieutenant Colonel John C. Walker of the 8th Texas, who had taken over from Wharton, redeployed the Confederates and opened a hot fire on the Federals to keep them pinned down behind their improvised breastworks.

Meanwhile, Morrison and Hood led a pell-mell charge into Murfreesboro. The prisoners in the jail heard the rescuers coming. One of the inmates was Confederate Army Captain William Richardson, an escapee from a prisoner-of-war camp who had been arrested traveling in civilian clothes and had been condemned as a spy. Richardson wrote later that he was "aroused from sleep by a strange noise like the roar of an approaching storm. The roar grew louder and came nearer, and in a very few seconds we were sure we could discern the clatter of horses' feet upon the hard turnpike. In a moment there could be no doubt as to the riders, for on the morning air there came the famous rebel yell."

While some of the raiders besieged the jail, others quickly overran the hotel, capturing General Crittenden and his staff. Nearby, a company of Michigan soldiers barricaded themselves inside the courthouse and opened fire on the Confederate attackers. The raiders charged the building from all sides as some of their number broke down the front door with an improvised battering-ram. The Confederates swarmed inside and quickly captured the defenders.

At the jail, the situation was precarious. The jail guards, realizing that they could not escape, nevertheless did not intend to sur-render their prisoners alive; they tried to shoot the Confederates in their cells. Captain Richardson and the others survived only by cringing into a nook in a forward corner of the cell where the guards could not bring their guns to bear.

But the captives were far from safe. "Before leaving the jail," Richardson later remembered, "one of the Federal guards struck a match and, lighting a bundle of papers, shoved them beneath the flooring. To our horror we realized that he was determined to burn us to death. When the Southern riders reached us the fire was already under good headway, and the jailer had fled with the keys."

The rescuers pried at a heavy metal door, managing to bend it enough to extricate the prisoners. Just as they escaped the burning building, Forrest rode up. According to the admiring Richardson, "his eyes were flashing as if on fire, his face was flushed, and he seemed in a condition of great excitement. To me he was the ideal of a warrior."

Meanwhile, Colonel Lawton had run into trouble to the west of town. The sound of gunfire from Murfreesboro had awakened Colonel Henry C. Lester in the Federal camp on Stones River, about a mile and a half from town. Lester immediately formed the 3rd Minnesota Infantry and the Kentucky Light Battery into a column and headed for the fighting. In a tree-bordered cornfield near the town, the Federals ran into Lawton's waiting Confederates. Swiftly deploying his battery, Lester shelled the Confederates, forcing them to pull back into the tree line on the east side of the field.

Lawton and his men were stalled there under fire when Forrest rode up. Sizing up the situation, he ordered the 1st Georgia, along

29

with a Tennessee and a Kentucky company, to ride around the Federals and burn their camp on the river. It was now 11 a.m., and some of Forrest's officers began to worry about Federal reinforcements arriving by train from Nashville. They proposed a withdrawal. "I didn't come here to make half a job of it," Forrest snapped. "I'm going to have them all."

Forrest devised a ruse. While his designated units circled Lester's position and attacked and set fire to the westernmost Feder-

al camp, Forrest rode back to where Colonel Parkhurst's troops lay pinned down behind their wagons and sent in a flag of truce. Forrest claimed to have captured all the other Federal troops in the area and demanded Parkhurst's surrender, adding that if his raiders had to attack they would take no prisoners. Parkhurst, thinking he was the last to hold out, surrendered at noon.

Forrest immediately returned to his troops at the cornfield and prepared another bluff. Ordering his men there to march back

Federal supply wagons trundle across a creek into Murfreesbor Tennessee, the target of Nathan ford Forrest's surprise attack. O July 13, 1862, Forrest's raiders c tured the Union garrison there a tore up the railroad tracks (*foreground*) that ran from the Federa base at nearby Nashville to the C federate bastion of Chattanooga.

With that, Forrest had them all — 1,200 prisoners, 50 wagons and teams, a battery of artillery and about a quarter of a million dollars' worth of assorted supplies. Before leaving, he destroyed the railroad depot and tore up the track near town. Since the loot was more than his troops could carry, Forrest made a deal with some of the prisoners: They would help haul the goods to McMinnville, and he would parole them to their homes.

Later, when General Buell heard of the wholesale surrender at Murfreesboro, he was outraged. "Few more disgraceful examples of neglect of duty and lack of good conduct can be found in the history of wars," Buell blustered. "It fully merits the extreme penalty for such misconduct."

But Buell had much greater problems. Lacking tight security at the many outposts along his extended line of supply and lacking the cavalry with which to chase down the raiders, he was forced yet again to delay his advance on Chattanooga to deal with the threats to his rear. He sent Brigadier General William (Bull) Nelson with a 3,500-man division to Murfreesboro to stop Forrest, repair the railroad there and keep it open.

Nelson's men repaired the railroad quickly, but they failed to stop Forrest or to keep the road open. On July 21 — the same day he was promoted to brigadier general — Forrest struck again, this time driving north of Murfreesboro, almost into Nashville. He destroyed three railroad bridges and took 97 prisoners. The railroad would be out of commission until July 29.

By that time, General Braxton Bragg at Tupelo had been prodded into an entirely new strategy and had set his army in motion toward an unexpected destination.

and forth in order to inflate their actual numbers in the eyes of the enemy, Forrest sent an intimidating note to Colonel Lester: "Colonel, I must demand an unconditional surrender of your force as prisoners of war or I will have every man put to the sword. You are aware of the overpowering force I have at my command, and this demand is made to prevent the effusion of blood." Thoroughly intimidated, Lester surrendered his 450 men and four guns.

Panic along the Ohio

"To arms!" the Cincinnati *Gazette* proclaimed in September 1862. "The time for playing war has passed. The enemy is approaching our doors." Indeed, the Confederate armies of Kirby Smith and Braxton Bragg were marching through Kentucky with little but raw Union recruits between them and the Ohio River ports of Louisville and Cincinnati. The citizens of these cities would have to defend themselves.

Major General Lew Wallace, in charge of Cincinnati's defense, declared martial law, threw a pontoon bridge across the river and sent 15,000 civilians to dig fortifications on the Kentucky side. From all over Ohio came a flood of volunteers, known as Squirrel Hunters for the muzzle-loading hunting rifles many of them carried. Wallace soon had 55,000 irregulars manning the earthworks and 16 impressed steamboats armed

with small cannon patrolling the riv . At Louisville, Kentucky, 130 mi downriver, General William Nelson a mobilized civilians in an attempt to ring city with earthworks, and he built brid to the Indiana shore — as much to evacu the city as to facilitate its defense. Me while, the Union Army of the Ohio, wh had driven deep into the South, raced no to intercept the oncoming Confederates

Union soldiers and a shirt-sleeve army of civilians cross the Ohio River on a makeshift bridge running alongside the abutments of a future span. The civilians —

The burghers of Cincinnati throng to enroll as laborers and as armed militiamen in the defense of their city. General Wallace had called for full mobilization with the slogan: "Citizens for labor, soldiers for battle."

Enrolling the Citizens

...ng parasols against the summer sun — used tools obtained from hardware stores to erect emergency fortifications around Covington, Kentucky (*background*).

Under the supervision of a mounted officer, soldiers and civilians in the hills south of Cincinnati fell trees for gun emplacements and dig trenches in anticipation of a Confederate attack. While the work progressed, all business in the city came to a halt, and even weddings and milk deliveries were postponed.

From a hilltop outside Covington, Kentucky, recruits of the newly formed 100th Ohio Volunteers guard the turnpike from Lexington. Confederate general Kirk

cupied Lexington, about 75 miles to the south, and had sent a column up the turnpike to probe the Union defenses.

In frantic flight, the people of Louisville jam the ferry docks on the Ohio River in a rush to evacuate their threatened city. During the crisis, Louisville, a city of

Refugees from Louisville, most of them women and children, huddle around campfires in relative safety on the north bank of the Ohio River. As a precaution, they had been ordered to flee their homes after Confederate cavalry raided the outskirts of the city on September 21, 1862.

e, was described by a reporter as a "howling uproar, filled with troops, teams, dust and the clatterbang of arms."

Winning the race to Louisville, a Federal relief column of 12,000 men — the advance division of the Army of the Ohio — trudges into the city on September 2

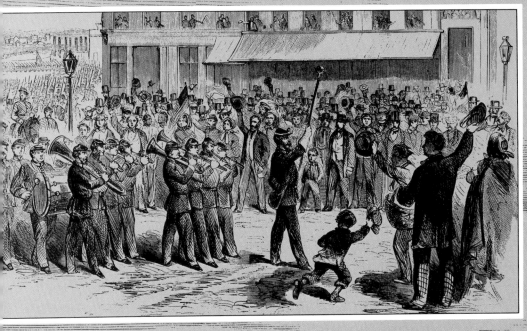

Cincinnati townspeople cheer their militia returning after the threat to the city was lifted. Following a week of raids and skirmishes, the Confederates had decided that Cincinnati's citizen-built defenses were too strong to risk an all-out attack.

ed march across the breadth of Kentucky. Bragg's Confederates were diverted east toward Perryville, Kentucky, and the battle for Louisville never materialized.

Stumbling toward Perryville

"Utter a shout of defiance against the Northern tyranny and proclaim that, under the guidance of heaven, Kentucky shall prove worthy of her ancient fame."

GENERAL SIMON BOLIVAR BUCKNER TO THE PEOPLE OF KENTUCKY, SEPTEMBER 24, 1862

It had been a fretful summer for the opposing army commanders intent on East Tennessee. With Confederate raiders continually nipping at the vulnerable Federal supply lines, General Buell's advance on Chattanooga had remained stalled in the vicinity of Decatur, Alabama, more than 100 miles west of his objective. On the Confederate side, General Bragg had reorganized and reinvigorated his army, situated in Tupelo roughly 100 miles southwest of Buell. But, characteristically, Bragg had seemed incapable of using his forces decisively; he had talked vaguely of striking northward into central Tennessee, but he had not moved. Neither had Kirby Smith, Bragg's junior, who had his headquarters 100 miles northeast of Chattanooga at Knoxville.

At the end of July 1862, however, the lull was about to end with a burst of activity that would race like a fast-burning fuse through eastern Tennessee and into the northern reaches of Kentucky. The rapid series of marches and countermarches, leading to a climactic battle at the village of Perryville, would be marked by error and confusion. Events would run their course, wildly beyond the control of either General Buell or General Bragg. Rather, these events would be shaped to a remarkable extent by the cunning Kirby Smith, who had paved the way for an invasion of Kentucky with a persistent and single-minded campaign of manipulation waged against his fellow officer, Braxton Bragg.

Smith was an ambitious, self-centered officer who had already enjoyed more than his share of fame. A graduate of West Point, he served with distinction in the Mexican War and later was wounded fighting Indians on the Western frontier. At the outbreak of the Civil War, he was a major in the 2nd U.S. Cavalry. But on April 6, 1861, his native state of Florida having seceded, Smith resigned his commission and entered the Confederate Army as a lieutenant colonel.

Smith served under General Joseph E. Johnston in the Shenandoah Valley and was quickly promoted to brigadier general. At Bull Run, his last-minute arrival on the field with his troops helped turn the tide for the Confederates and won him instant fame. When the young hero married, his wife was dubbed "The Bride of the Confederacy."

After all the accolades in the first year of the War, the aggressive, 38-year-old Smith resented his assignment to a small western department with little scope for action. But he soon conceived an invasion of Kentucky as a way to relieve his boredom — and to bring himself glory. However, he could not move north while he was chained to the defense of Chattanooga. To free himself for the invasion, Smith would have to persuade others to assume the responsibility of protecting the city; this project he undertook with energy and determination.

Beginning in the last week of June, he sent off a spate of alarming messages describing the danger posed to Chattanooga by Buell's

for militia, claiming: "My force is not sufficient to defend this department." On June 26, he wired General Robert E. Lee that the enemy threatened Chattanooga and that reinforcements should be rushed. The next day he reported Buell's approach to General Bragg, with the complaint, "I have no force to repel such an attack." It was then that Bragg reluctantly sent a division of 3,000 men under Major General John P. McCown to Chattanooga.

Still the alarms continued. "Large reinforcements speedily forwarded can alone save Chattanooga," Smith hectored the War Department on June 28. And on July 2, the day after Henry Heth arrived with his troops, Smith reported darkly that the enemy was ready to cross the Tennessee River: "Their attack may be daily looked for."

But Smith's military dispositions never reflected the concern that he repeatedly expressed. While fretting about the danger to Chattanooga, he had kept 9,000 of his best troops under his most capable commander, Brigadier General Carter L. Stevenson, posted north of Knoxville; there they faced Brigadier General George W. Morgan's 10,000 Federals in the Cumberland Gap. Indeed, only 9,000 Confederates, most of them raw recruits, remained in Chattanooga to oppose Buell's 31,000-man Army of the Ohio. Moreover, Smith placed General McCown in command, despite Bragg's warning that McCown lacked "capacity and nerve for a separate, responsible command."

On July 10, Smith again warned Bragg that Buell was drawing closer and then, as if the threat to Chattanooga were no longer his concern, Smith announced, "I am mobilizing my command for movement on General Morgan or into Middle Tennessee, as the cir-

advance and his own inability to withstand an attack. On June 24, Smith warned the War Department, "If the Government wishes Chattanooga secured, a reinforcement of at least 2,000 armed men must be immediately sent there and an officer of ability assigned to the command." President Jefferson Davis himself replied the next day that Brigadier General Henry Heth was on his way, along with 6,000 reinforcements.

Smith was far from satisfied. On June 25, he wrote to the Governor of Georgia pleading

cumstances may demand." Three days previously, he had sent a confidential letter to General Stevenson outlining his real purpose — to outflank Morgan and drive into Kentucky. But Smith was not yet ready to reveal his plan to anyone else.

On July 14, he sent a long letter to President Davis detailing his dispositions and organization but not his intentions. He warned Davis that Buell's army constituted "an overwhelming force, that cannot be resisted except by Bragg's cooperation."

Bragg, meanwhile, had been beset by problems. General Grant was advancing toward Vicksburg, and Bragg had been compelled to send considerable forces westward to aid in the defense of the city. His army at Tupelo was now desperately short of men, food and supplies.

The movement northward that Bragg had contemplated seemed increasingly doubtful. He lacked the wagons and teams needed to supply his troops on the march. And to make matters worse, drought had so parched the countryside that his men would be unable to find food, forage or even water. While Bragg grappled with these concerns, Smith hammered away, sending him on July 19 yet another warning coupled with another attempt to shift responsibility: Buell, Smith wrote, "was momentarily expected to attack. If possible hasten your movement on East Tennessee. The successful holding of Chattanooga depends upon your cooperation."

The next day, Bragg replied, "We are fearfully outnumbered in this department. I have hoped you would be able to cope with General Buell's force, especially as he would have to cross a broad and deep river in your immediate presence. That hope still exists; but I must urge on you the propriety of your

taking command in Chattanooga. The officer I sent you, I regret to say, cannot be trusted with such a command, and I implore you not to entrust him indeed with any important position."

Taking command at Chattanooga was precisely what Kirby Smith did not want to do. McCown would remain in charge there; and Smith ignored the suggestion, continuing his relentless series of messages. On July 20, he told Bragg that Buell's attack "may be hourly expected. It is your time to strike."

With that, Kirby Smith won his game. The next day, Bragg went into motion. Leaving forces under Generals Earl Van Dorn and Sterling Price in northern Mississippi to deal with Grant, he ordered the Army of the Mississippi to Chattanooga.

It was a difficult movement around Buell's interposing army, but Bragg, despite his problems, managed the logistics magnificently. He sent his mounted units — the cavalry, artillery and wagon trains, about 5,000 men in all — overland by a 430-mile route south to Tuscaloosa, Alabama, east to Rome, Georgia, then north to Chattanooga. Because of the supply problems and the drought, the 35,000 infantrymen had to be moved by train, and that involved a journey of almost 800 miles — south all the way to Mobile, Alabama, then east to Atlanta, Georgia, and thence northwest to Chattanooga.

The first elements entrained on July 23. Commissary agents met the trains at intervals to reprovision the men. Transfer points were closely guarded to prevent soldiers from straying. And there were many transfers; the movement involved six railroads of different gauges, a ferry across Mobile Bay and a steamboat up a stretch of the Alabama

General Edmund Kirby Smith, and modest in manner with his officers, revealed a driving am in correspondence with his w one letter, Smith compared hi with Cortez, in another with M and he predicted that his cam in Kentucky would be hai the Confederate press as "a s of inspiration and gen

River to Montgomery. The advance elements reached Chattanooga on July 27, two days before the last train left Tupelo.

But Bragg, having moved his army, still had to decide what to do with it. He told the War Department, rather tentatively, "I hope in conjunction with Major General Smith to strike an effective blow through Middle Tennessee, gaining the enemy's rear, cutting off his supplies and dividing his forces, so as to encounter him in detail." But Bragg's natural indecisiveness was accentuated by his feeling that he was an interloper in Smith's Department of East Tennessee; this reluc-

tance to act, combined with his dour reticence, left him no match for the younger man's steely determination.

Instead of taking command of their combined operations, Bragg treated Smith as an equal and independent commander. In a meeting in Chattanooga on July 31, as Bragg later explained to his superiors in Richmond, they "arranged measures for mutual support and effective cooperation" — a time-honored prescription for military disaster.

The course of action on which they agreed was simple and sound enough, as far as it went: Since Bragg's mounted units had not yet arrived, he could not take the field; Smith would move immediately against General Morgan's Federals in the Cumberland Gap. If Morgan was driven off and if by that time Bragg's wagon trains had arrived, the two generals would combine their forces and move into central Tennessee to cut off Buell.

The strategy was left vague enough to satisfy both generals — Bragg, whose objective was Buell's army, and Smith, who never wavered from the course he had charted into Kentucky. A few days after the Chattanooga meeting, Smith pleaded for reinforcements from Bragg, who obligingly sent two of his best brigades under Brigadier General Patrick R. Cleburne and Colonel Preston Smith. Bragg now had only 27,000 men to confront Buell's entire army, while Smith had in excess of 20,000 troops to take on General Morgan's lone division.

Bragg tried to redress the imbalance by ordering that Major General John C. Breckinridge's division be detached from Van Dorn's department and sent east to him.

But Kirby Smith had a plan, and on August 9 he began to put it into effect. Ostensibly describing his implementation of the agreement, he detailed his preparations for moving against Morgan. Then came an artful qualification: "I understand General Morgan has at Cumberland Gap nearly a month's supply of provisions. If this be true then the reduction of the place would be a matter of more time than I presume you are willing I should take. As my move direct to Lexington, Kentucky, would effectually invest Morgan and would be attended with other most brilliant results in my judgment, I suggest I be allowed to take that course."

Bragg, reluctant to countermand Kirby Smith, acceded with a minor reservation. "It would be unadvisable, I think, for you to move far into Kentucky, leaving Morgan in your rear, until I am able to fully engage Buell and his forces on your left."

With these words, Bragg lost control of his campaign before it began. On August 14, leaving Carter Stevenson's division to face Morgan in the Cumberland Gap, Smith marched eagerly out of Knoxville with 6,000 men — three divisions under Heth, General Cleburne and Brigadier General Thomas J. Churchill. The previous day Smith had sent his cavalry, commanded by Colonel John S. Scott, on a wide sweep ahead of his route.

Laboriously, the column worked its way northwest, onto the plateau of the Cumberland Mountains, and then turned northeast, bypassing Morgan's troops in the Cumberland Gap. It was a hard march through a mountainous land parched by the drought. There was little foraging, and the supply wagons lagged far behind Smith's infantry. On August 18, Smith wrote his wife proudly, "Our men have marched night and day, and have carried their own subsistence in their haversacks for five days. Ragged, barefoot, they have climbed mountains, suffered star-

A torn recruiting poster issued by General Kirby Smith urges Kentuckians to enlist in his Confederate forces, promising that divisions commanded by two of the state's most admired men, Generals John C. Breckinridge and Simon Bolivar Buckner, were about to arrive.

vation and thirst without a murmur." On that day they swarmed into Barboursville, Kentucky, squarely in Morgan's rear and athwart his supply line to Lexington. Morgan, realizing he had been outflanked, would soon evacuate the Cumberland Gap, withdrawing his forces into eastern Kentucky.

On August 20, Smith announced that he was going on to Lexington, where he could get supplies. As an afterthought he explained that he would thus provide a diversion for Bragg's operations against Buell. Again Bragg meekly accepted Smith's declaration.

In fact, Smith had little reason for confidence; his men were weary, short of supplies and harassed by bushwhackers. Behind them was Morgan's hostile army and ahead of them a Federal force of unknown size. To make matters worse, on August 24, Colonel Scott sent bad news. While ranging up the road toward Lexington, Scott's troopers had run into Federal cavalry atop Big Hill, on the western edge of the Cumberland Mountains.

The Federal troops consisted of the 7th Kentucky Cavalry and a battalion of the 3rd Tennessee Cavalry, commanded by Colonel Leonidas Metcalfe. At Scott's approach, Colonel Metcalfe ordered a charge. As the army's adjutant general, J. Mills Kendrick, reported later, Metcalfe then "had the mortification to find that not more than 100 of his regiment followed him; the remainder, at the first cannon shot, turned tail and fled like a pack of cowards." A few men from the 3rd Tennessee rescued their commander.

Scott chased the Federals up the road to Richmond, Kentucky, 20 miles southeast of Lexington. But during the chase, the Confederate troopers learned from a captured dispatch that heavy Federal reinforcements were due in Richmond by August 23.

Smith had not expected enemy resistance so soon, but he could not postpone his advance on Lexington. Taking the town was now his only hope of getting supplies.

Smith informed Bragg on August 24 that he would push on. At the same time, he made a startling proposal: Bragg should move north across the Cumberland Mountains to distract Buell's Federals from Smith's operations. Smith wanted an additional 3,000 men, from Brigadier General Humphrey Marshall's Department of Western Virginia, to join him in an advance to the banks of the Ohio. Smith did not explain what they were going to do when they got there; but Bragg, astonishingly, swallowed the idea. Still behaving like a subordinate, he compliantly began moving his Army of the Mississippi northward from Chattanooga toward Kentucky on August 28.

On the following day, Smith set out for Lexington with his forces. On August 29, they crossed Big Hill and moved into the rolling hills that bordered Kentucky's lush Bluegrass country. But late in the afternoon, Scott's advance guard ran into an aggressive Federal cavalry force — Colonel Metcalfe again, but with better men under his command. Metcalfe drove Scott's troopers back into the midst of the leading Confederate infantry units, part of Cleburne's division. "Yelling as though they were all excited with liquor," as Cleburne reported later, the Federal cavalry dismounted to face the Confederate infantry fire. The skirmish continued until dark; then the Federals withdrew toward the town of Richmond.

Smith made plans for an early-morning attack. Although he was told that he was facing eight regiments and was slightly outnumbered, he was encouraged when he discovered that most of the Federal troops were raw recruits hastily assembled in Louisville a few days before; and he would rather fight them at Richmond than at Lexington, where the high bluffs of the Kentucky River would greatly favor the defenders.

Apparently the Federal decision to make a stand in Richmond was based on poor timing. During the night, Brigadier General Mahlon D. Manson, commanding the Federal infantry at Richmond, sent a courier to Lexington for instructions from his superior officer. Major General William Nelson, who weighed 300 pounds and carried the nickname Bull, had been sent north two weeks earlier to take charge of affairs in Kentucky. When the messenger reached him at 2:30 a.m., Nelson advised retreat; but Manson received the reply too late. Meanwhile Nelson, who had little confidence in the green troops arrayed at Richmond, got dressed and headed out to take command himself.

August 30 dawned clear and beautiful. Scott's cavalrymen had located four Federal infantry regiments with artillery across the Lexington Pike on high ground seven miles south of Richmond. The other Federal regiments were still marching south on the pike.

Cleburne moved his division into position but delayed his attack until Churchill's division arrived. To occupy the enemy in the meantime, Cleburne ordered his artillery — Captain James P. Douglas' Texas Battery and the Marion Light Artillery — to "fire very slowly and not waste a round."

The Federals, with the 55th Indiana in the lead, began to advance toward the Confederate right. They were met by the men of the 154th Tennessee, who held until the rest of the Confederate brigade under Colonel Preston Smith moved up in support. Then, at about 7:30 a.m., Kirby Smith arrived with Churchill's division. Kirby Smith immediately ordered Colonel T. H. McCray's brigade of Arkansas and Texas troops to move to the left and attack the Federal right.

McCray moved into position, his lines overlapping the Federal right flank. Ignoring this threat, the Federal infantry closed with the Confederates on Cleburne's right flank, only to be repulsed with heavy casualties by the men of Preston Smith's brigade. Cleburne was wounded in the mouth by a bullet and had to leave the field. Colonel Smith took command of the division.

Now on the defensive, the green Federal troops were still fighting well. They fell back on the left and re-formed their lines, only to break again when McCray's brigade smashed into their right. Three late-arriving Federal regiments were caught in the rout as their comrades ran toward Richmond.

General Nelson arrived on the field about 2 p.m. and managed to re-form about 2,200 of his men for a last stand on a ridge just south of the town. It was a formidable position, its left anchored on a stone wall in the Richmond cemetery, its right in a nearly impenetrable thicket.

The weary Confederates, who had been fighting all day without water, attacked again at 5 p.m. McCray's brigade charged the Federal right under heavy fire, while the men of Cleburne's division scrambled up the slope of the ridge into the Federal center and left. Urged on by Preston Smith, Cleburne's men quickly swarmed over the stone wall and engaged the Federal defenders in hand-to-hand combat among the tombstones of the cemetery. Churchill's men, meanwhile, poured into the thicket on the Federal right. In no time at all, Nelson's Federals were in full flight. As Nelson later wrote, "Our troops stood about three rounds, then struck by a panic, they fled in utter disorder." The Federals raced back through the town and onto the Lexington road — into a trap.

Earlier in the afternoon, Kirby Smith had sent Scott's cavalry on a wide sweep to get behind the Federal position. When the rout began, Scott was ready; the fleeing soldiers ran straight into a barrage from Confederate horse artillery. Fully half the Federal troops laid down their arms and surrendered.

With a loss of 78 killed and 372 wounded, the Confederates had captured more than 4,000 Federal troops, 10,000 stands of arms, nine guns and a complete wagon train carrying all of the enemy's supplies. Nelson, who had been wounded and captured but who soon escaped, reported a Federal toll of 206 killed and 844 wounded.

Kirby Smith now faced no real opposition in the Bluegrass or eastern Kentucky. Smith triumphantly moved his headquarters to Lexington and sent a cavalry force to occupy the state capital at Frankfort. The Confeder-

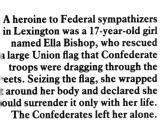

ates had an open road all the way to the Ohio River, and the citizens of Cincinnati were in agonies of fear. General Lew Wallace was rushed to that city to draft civilians and lash together a makeshift defense. President Lincoln, even while preoccupied with disaster much closer to home — Lee's defeat of General Pope at Second Bull Run — took time to ask fretfully the whereabouts of General Buell. Meanwhile Kirby Smith, established in Kentucky at last, suddenly ran out of ideas. He went on the defensive and waited to see what Bragg and Buell were going to do.

General Buell had spent June and July feeling sorry for himself, bemoaning what he later called "the crippling of an invading army by a successful war upon its too long and inadequately protected communica-

tions." By August 1, the sorely distracted general had been told that Bragg had arrived in Chattanooga with 80,000 to 100,000 troops for an assault on Nashville. Buell planned to withdraw from his exposed position along the south bank of the Tennessee as soon as he was sure of Bragg's intentions. In the meantime, he managed to persuade Federal General in Chief Henry W. Halleck to send him two divisions from Grant's army.

By stationing troops at vital points along his supply line, Buell was able to repel Confederate raiders south of the Cumberland. But to the north, as Buell wrote, "the depredations were prosecuted with increased vigor. Our cavalry was totally insufficient to cope with these incursions, which it must be said, also, were seldom resisted by the infantry guards with vigilance and resolution."

On August 12, for example, Confederate raiders under John Hunt Morgan swept into Gallatin, Tennessee, a town on the vital railroad between Nashville and the Federal supply center at Louisville. After the Confederates captured the garrison, burned the depot and destroyed some trestles, they turned their attention to an 800-foot railroad tunnel that had been cut through a mountain north of the town. Morgan's men set fire to a captured train loaded with hay and pushed it into the tunnel; the timber supports caught fire and burned until the tunnel collapsed.

With the railroad now closed for months and Kirby Smith on the move into Kentucky, Buell began debating whether he should withdraw toward Nashville or confront the Confederates somewhere else in central Tennessee. In the end he decided to concentrate the Army of the Ohio at McMinnville, on the Cumberland Plateau northwest of Chattanooga, where he would

49

be in position to block any advance by Bragg.

It turned out to be the right move. Bragg crossed the Tennessee River at Chattanooga on August 28 and began his march north to Kentucky, heading up the Sequatchie Valley to Pikeville and then across the Cumberland Plateau toward Sparta, just 20 miles northeast of McMinnville.

Bragg's troops were now within easy striking distance, but Buell did not attack, despite the urgings of his senior division commander, Major General George H. Thomas. The muddled reports of the Confederate movement confused and alarmed Buell, and instead of closing with Bragg, he withdrew westward to Murfreesboro, 35 miles southeast of Nashville.

Buell arrived at Murfreesboro on September 5 and learned of Kirby Smith's occupation of Lexington. Concluding that Bragg must be aiming for Nashville, Buell started his army toward that city.

Buell's supply situation was growing worse. He wrote later that he was "now reduced to ten days' provisions. Our railroad communications north of Nashville had been broken for twenty days, and no effort was being made in Louisville to reopen it."

About 50 miles east of Buell, meanwhile, Bragg's leading wing, under Major General Leonidas Polk, emerged from the Cumberland Mountains at Sparta and headed north. Bragg had ordered Polk to march to Glasgow, Kentucky, seize the Louisville & Nashville Railroad line there and then wait for the arrival of the army's other wing under Major General William J. Hardee.

Once again Bragg demonstrated his ability to move an army smartly — although as he marched, Bragg had not yet decided exactly where he was going. But he knew he must

Commander of one wing of Braxton Bragg's army, William Joseph Hardee was beloved by his troops because his concern for their welfare. Hardee was so "kind and considerate," one observer reported, that he would "give up his horse to some barefoot or sick soldier and walk for miles."

prevent Buell from getting between him and Kirby Smith. So while Buell withdrew in confusion to Nashville, the Army of the Mississippi drove northward.

Buoyed by the news of General Smith's victory at Lexington, the morale of Bragg's Confederates was running high — in no small measure because of the warm reception they got from Kentuckians. Private Sam Watkins of the 1st Tennessee wrote later, "I thought they had the prettiest girls that God ever made. They could not do too much for us. They had heaps and stacks of cooked rations along our route, with wine and cider everywhere, and the glad shouts of 'Hurrah for our Southern boys!' greeted and welcomed us at every house. Ah, the boys felt like soldiers again. The bands played 'Dixie' and 'Bonnie Blue Flag,' the citizens cheered, and the ladies waved their handkerchiefs and threw us bouquets."

The footsore Confederates marched into

Glasgow on September 14. Buell, meanwhile, had received word of the Confederate advance northward and had pushed through Nashville with his troops on a parallel route; his main force reached Bowling Green, 30 miles west of Glasgow, on September 14.

Bragg's movement had forced the Army of the Ohio out of Alabama and central Tennessee without a battle, but soon, by accident, the Federals would be drawn into combat. By the time Bragg reached Glasgow, he had changed his mind again, deciding against joining Kirby Smith at Lexington. Instead, he now determined to involve Smith in a joint movement against Louisville — a rich prize. That city was the Federal supply center for Kentucky and Tennessee, and its loss would cripple Buell's operations. Bragg also hoped the fall of such a major city on the Ohio River would stimulate the Confederate recruitment he had been awaiting in vain.

Almost immediately, the new plan ran into a snag. While his troops were still marching into Glasgow, Bragg sent Brigadier General James R. Chalmers with his Mississippi brigade 10 miles to the north to cut the Louisville & Nashville Railroad line at Cave City. Chalmers accomplished the mission with ease, but he then made the mistake of embarking on an additional, unauthorized attack on Munfordville, farther up the railroad. Misinformed as to the size of the 4,000-man Federal garrison there, Chalmers was repulsed with a loss of 35 killed and 253 wounded. Bragg, doubly furious at Chalmers — for disregarding orders and for then being defeated — sent Hardee's troops to Munfordville and Polk's circling to the Federal rear. The Federal garrison was surrounded by midafternoon on September 16.

Bragg expected a quick surrender, but he had brought the wrong man to bay. Colonel John T. Wilder of the 17th Indiana Volunteers was a wily and stubborn officer. Told that he was surrounded by 20,000 men, Wilder demanded evidence. Bragg replied that he would provide proof when he attacked. Wilder asked to talk things over and Bragg agreed, allowing Wilder to tour the Confederate lines. After counting 46 cannon trained on his defenses, Wilder decided it would not be dishonorable to surrender. But there were questions of procedure to discuss, and he would not agree to march his men out of the town until 6 a.m. on the 17th.

Bragg's move to Louisville had been delayed for two full days, yet he felt no sense of urgency. Assuming that Buell's army would remain in Bowling Green and apparently quite unconcerned about word that a strong Federal force was digging in at Louisville, Bragg gave his army a day off to celebrate its first victory of the campaign. Then

Federal troops in formation make their way across a bridge over the Big Barren River near Bowling Green, Kentucky. Recently repaired by the use of po

round), the span served as a vital link in General Buell's Louisville-to-Nashville supply line.

he learned that Buell was on the move.

There were compelling reasons now for both generals to fight. Bragg had gained Buell's rear, had cut the Federal line of communications, had won a small but bracing victory and now occupied a strong defensive position on the Green River's banks. Buell, on the other hand, enjoyed numerical superiority and had a chance to deal with Bragg before Kirby Smith could reinforce him.

But neither general had the nerve to press the issue. Buell made a tentative move toward Munfordville on September 18. Bragg went into agonies of sleepless indecision for two days; then he marched northeast to Bardstown, where he had asked Smith to send supplies and join him. Somewhat lamely, Bragg declared that "this campaign must be won by marching, not fighting." Buell seemed to agree, for when he found the road to the north abandoned by Bragg's forces, he marched north with unaccustomed speed and arrived in Louisville on September 25.

When Bragg arrived in Bardstown, he found that Kirby Smith had neither sent supplies nor even left Lexington. Seemingly uninterested in any campaign not of his own making, Smith simply decided that Bragg could take Louisville on his own, and Smith stayed where he was. But Bragg had left Munfordville with only three days' provisions and now had to scatter his men across the parched countryside to find food.

Buell was unable to take advantage of the Confederate disarray; his arrival in Louisville had plunged him into a series of complications and disasters. For one thing, he now found himself in yet another military district—that of General H. G. Wright. And so, while the citizens of Louisville neared a state of panic and General Nelson labored to

bring raw recruits into some semblance of effectiveness, Buell had to contend with Wright over who was in charge in the area. Buell finally confirmed with General in Chief Halleck that he was indeed in command.

Then Buell lost one of his favorite officers. In a pointless argument, General Nelson was shot in the chest by Brigadier General Jefferson C. Davis. Nelson died a half hour later. Davis was arrested immediately and handed over to the civil authorities. He was indicted, but in the press of the military campaign, he was not brought to trial. He was soon restored to command of his division.

To make matters worse for Buell, President Lincoln chose this time to express his dismay over the general's failure to contest the Confederate advance to the Ohio River. On September 24, at the President's insistence, Halleck had dispatched an aide with orders for Buell to turn over his command to one of his senior divisional commanders, Major General George H. Thomas. But then Halleck learned that Buell had become something of a hero—in fact, he was being regarded as the man who had saved Louisville and Cincinnati. Halleck now had second thoughts about firing him; he quickly wired the messenger not to deliver the orders, but it was too late. General Thomas resolved the embarrassing situation by refusing the command on the ground that Buell's preparations to march against the enemy had been completed. Buell retained his post, with Thomas as his second-in-command.

Buell seemed determined to make the most of his second chance. After assimilating the green Louisville garrison into his army as best he could, he had 60,000 troops, and on October 1 he put them on a collision course with the Confederates. Three corps—each with three divisions — under Generals Alexander McCook, T. L. Crittenden and Charles Gilbert marched by separate routes southeast toward Bardstown and Bragg's Army of the Mississippi.

Buell intended, he said, "to force the enemy's left back and compel him to concentrate as far as possible from any convenient line of retreat, while at the same time making a strong demonstration against his right, so as to mislead him as to the real point of attack." General Joshua Sills was to take a division toward Frankfort to provide the diversion. Another division, under Brigadier

General William W. Dumont, would follow.

After two months of confusion, the contending forces in Kentucky were at last steeling themselves for confrontation. And Braxton Bragg was not with his army.

First Kirby Smith and then Braxton Bragg had predicated the success of their invasion on the recruiting of thousands of Kentuckians. It had not come to pass. Smith had managed to scrape together less than a brigade of new volunteers, and Bragg had garnered not a one. When Smith refused to come to Bardstown as requested, Bragg went to Lexington

NEW YORK
ILLUSTRATED NEWS.

No. 154.—Vol. VI.   NEW-YORK, SATURDAY, OCTOBER 18, 1862.   Price Six Cents.

THE SHOOTING OF GENERAL NELSON, AT THE GALT HOUSE, LOUISVILLE, KY., BY GEN. JEFF. C. DAVIS. From a Sketch by our Special Artist, J. C. Beard. See page 371.

A contemporary newspaper shows General Jefferson Davis firing a pistol shot into the chest of his superior, General William Nelson, after an argument over Davis' performance. Davis, a native of Indiana, a staunch Unionist and no relation to his namesake, the Confederacy's President, had served gallantly as a volunteer in the Mexican War and was stationed at Fort Sumter during the bombardment that began the Civil War. After shooting Nelson, Davis was arrested and indicted but because of the urgency of the military situation, he was never brought to trial

to discuss their next move. There the younger general airily observed that Bragg would have to defeat Buell before there would be any rush to the Confederate ranks.

But Bragg came up with a less militant idea; he would stimulate recruitment and create a legal framework for conscription in the state by ceremoniously installing a Confederate governor of Kentucky in Frankfort, the state capital. There was some basis for such a move: The state had been accepted into the Confederacy in 1861, and a provisional government had been set up, only to be driven south by Federal forces. The Provisional Governor had been killed at Shiloh, but the Lieutenant Governor, Richard Hawes, was available to assume the office.

Thus as the bulk of the Federal Army of the Ohio approached Bardstown, Bragg was away from his headquarters, preoccupied with the staging of an elaborate inaugural ceremony. To make matters worse, his troops were in disarray. He had reclaimed Cleburne's and Preston Smith's divisions, and his army now numbered 22,500. But they were scattered along a 50-mile front from Bardstown northeast to Shelbyville, halfway between Louisville and Frankfort.

On October 2, Bragg learned that a large Federal force had taken Shelbyville, driving Cleburne's division back toward Frankfort. This was Buell's feint, and Bragg responded to it just as the Federals had hoped. He sent word to Kirby Smith to bring up his 10,000-man force from Lexington and ordered General Polk, in command of the forces at Bardstown, to march northward immediately and strike the Federals on the right flank as they advanced toward Frankfort.

Polk knew better. His cavalry had told him that the Federals were moving south toward Bardstown in force. By the morning of October 2, all three of the main roads leading to Bardstown were clogged with blueclad columns. Acidly replying to Bragg's order, Polk said that compliance would be "not only eminently inexpedient but impracticable." Instead, he would fall back toward Bryantsville, where a supply depot had been set up earlier and a reserve force waited.

Incredibly, with most of his army in retreat, Bragg left matters in the hands of his subordinates and pressed on with the inauguration, scheduled for October 4 in Frankfort. But despite Bragg's single-minded determination, the ceremony was less than successful; at the end of Hawes's address, the affair was broken up by the sound of guns in the distance to the west. Now the mercurial Bragg decided he was being attacked by the entire Army of the Ohio, so he abandoned Frankfort to the Federals and hurried south to join Polk. The Hawes Administration's tenure had lasted about eight hours.

At this point, the Confederate forces in Kentucky were divided. Polk and Hardee were falling back to the southeast from Bardstown, pressed hard by Federal cavalry. Polk was on the Springfield Pike, while Hardee took a parallel route about 10 miles to the west, struggling to keep up over terrible roads. Meanwhile Kirby Smith was moving south from Frankfort. A bystander noted that a passing column of Confederates appeared "distressed, weary and harassed."

Now Bragg decided that his scattered forces should concentrate at Harrodsburg, 10 miles northwest of Danville and more than 20 miles east of Hardee's location. From there Bragg intended to turn northward and meet Buell's army, which he persisted in believing was converging on Frankfort. The inevitable battle would be fought, he decided, between Frankfort and Harrodsburg, in the vicinity of Versailles. He ordered Kirby Smith to halt his troops north of the Kentucky River, near Versailles, to watch for the route of the Federal advance.

As they maneuvered through the rolling Kentucky hills, troops on both sides suffered from the worsening drought. They grew desperate for water and had to take it wherever they could find it. A man of the 50th Ohio wrote: "The boys got some water out of a dark pond one night and used it at supper to make their coffee and to quench their thirst also. What was their disgust next morning to find a dead mule or two in the pond. I imagine that coffee had a rich flavor."

In a message to Polk on October 5, Hardee complained of his difficulty in maintaining the pace over the "hilly, rocky and slippery" terrain. Polk responded by ordering Hardee to cross to the Springfield road and fall in behind Polk's columns. This fateful move cost Hardee a day's march toward Harrodsburg and put his rear guard under heavy pressure from the Federal advance. Report-

A Son of Virginia on the Union Side

Brigadier General William Rufus Terrill (*right*), who commanded a Federal brigade in Jackson's division at Perryville, saw his family torn asunder by the War. Virginia-born and a relative of both Jeb Stuart and Robert E. Lee, Terrill nevertheless remained faithful to his oath as a U.S. officer, pledged when he graduated from West Point in 1853. The decision to fight for the Union outraged his father, who wrote Terrill a heart-scalding letter: "Can you be so recreant and so unnatural as to aid in the mad attempt to impose the yoke of tyranny upon your kith and kin? Do so and your name shall be stricken from the family records."

Despite the pain caused by the family rupture, Terrill proved a brilliant officer, especially distinguishing himself as an artillerist at the Battle of Shiloh. "Wherever Captain Terrill turned his battery," a Shiloh veteran recalled, "silence followed on the part of the enemy." Promoted to brigadier general, Terrill was commanding infantry in battle for the first time at Perryville when he was killed by a Confederate shell.

Terrill's only brother, James, was also killed in the War while serving with General Lee's Confederate Army of Northern Virginia. After the conflict, the Terrill family erected a memorial to the dead brothers on which is carved, "God Alone Knows Which Was Right."

ing the harassment the next day, Hardee was instructed by Polk to halt in order to "force the enemy to reveal his strength."

Hardee's trailing division, 7,000 men under Major General Simon Bolivar Buckner, was then at Perryville. Hardee placed the brigades of Brigadier Generals S.A.M. Wood and Bushrod Johnson on a ridge north of the town, while the five veteran Arkansas regiments of Brigadier General St. John Liddell took their place on a low range of hills west of the town overlooking a shallow creek — now dry — called Bull Run.

During the next day, the drought became a factor in the selection of a battlefield. The thirsty Confederates had come across some pools of precious water in the bed of Doctor's Creek, another mile west of Liddell's line. This watercourse, over which blood would soon be shed, ran roughly north-south and was bracketed by two parallel ridges. On the afternoon of October 7, two of Liddell's regiments — the 5th and 7th Arkansas — pushed out from their line to take up a position on the ridge east of Doctor's Creek. There the men listened to the sounds of skirmishing coming ever closer as units of Brigadier General Joseph Wheeler's cavalry, ranging farther to the west, encountered the advancing Federal cavalry screen, exchanged shots and fell back.

On the afternoon of the 7th, Hardee requested reinforcements and permission to drive off the Federals in order to end their harassment and give Bragg more time to concentrate the army. Bragg responded by further dividing his forces, sending Polk back from Harrodsburg with Major General Benjamin F. Cheatham's single division to help Hardee deal with the Federals at Perryville. The rest of the army continued to prepare for a fight 20 miles away, at Versailles.

Meanwhile Buell, as confused as Bragg, concluded that the entire Confederate army was in front of him at Perryville. Nursing a painful gash in his leg, suffered in a fall from his horse, Buell lurched from place to place in an ambulance, urging his corps commanders to concentrate their forces. All day on October 7 the Federal columns approached Perryville from the west on three separate roads. Gilbert's corps, in the Federal center, led the way on the Springfield Pike. About eight miles behind, to the north, McCook's corps marched on the Mackville Pike. And Crittenden's corps trailed 10 miles behind Gilbert on the Lebanon Pike to the south.

In the narrowing gap between the marching Federals and the waiting Confederates, contesting cavalry detachments from both armies seesawed back and forth. Late in the afternoon, troopers of the 9th Pennsylvania and 2nd Michigan Cavalry of Captain Ebenezer Gay's brigade finally drove the persistent — and by now thoroughly exhausted — Confederate cavalry back through Liddell's advanced regiments on the ridge. The hot and thirsty Federal troopers made a dash for the water in Doctor's Creek but were driven back by fire from the Arkansas troops. Then Gilbert's divisions approached the creek at about 11 p.m., and they wanted water.

The advanced brigades were part of a division commanded by Philip Sheridan, who was exceedingly proud of his new brigadier general's stars and was determined to prove himself worthy of them. He was about to get his chance. Almost immediately on arrival, the 10th Indiana of Brigadier General Speed Fry's brigade advanced to feel out the Confederate position and seize the creek bed. But when the regiment collided with the determined 7th Arkansas, the Indiana men were forced to fall back.

General Buell, who was traveling with Gilbert around 2 a.m., not far behind the leading units, learned of the repulse and ordered another attack. Sheridan advanced two regiments from the brigade of Colonel Daniel McCook — brother of Alexander McCook, the corps commander. Moving out cautiously along the Springfield Pike, McCook's men descended the slope west of the creek, crossed the watercourse and made their way up the slope on the far side. Under what McCook recalled as "a severe and galling fire," they exploded upon the Confederate line. Liddell's veterans fought well, but they were unable to check the momentum of the thirsty Federals. Under relentless pressure, the Arkansans were forced to abandon their position and withdraw east toward Perryville.

General Gilbert now became worried that Sheridan might advance too far and cautioned him against bringing on a general engagement before the army's other two corps were in position. As Sheridan later recalled it, he replied "that I was not bringing on an engagement but that the enemy evidently intended to do so." He nonetheless heeded the warning and stopped his advance on the ridge just east of Doctor's Creek; soon Gilbert began moving reinforcements forward to Sheridan's exposed position.

Although Sherman was vulnerable to flanking attacks, he now held one of the key positions on the battlefield. What is more, he had secured a water supply. This meant little, however, to the columns of thirsty Federal infantrymen who continued to trudge through the night toward Perryville. "Hour after hour we plodded on in the darkness," recalled Wilbur F. Hinman, an officer of the

65th Ohio Volunteers. "It was a dewless night and there was not a breath of wind to scatter the dust that hung in heavy clouds about us and settled on our clothing, completely covering us in a mantle of white."

During the night, Polk had marched into Perryville with Cheatham's division and had taken command of the Confederate forces. His orders from Bragg were to attack the next morning. Although no one on either

In a cornfield on the far left of the Federal line at Perryville, men of the 21st Wisconsin level a volley at General George E. Maney's Confederate brigade advancing through the stalks. The Wisconsin men, along with three other regiments of General John C. Starkweather's brigade, prevented the Confederates from turning the Federal flank.

side understood the situation, there were now 16,000 Confederates in Perryville, preparing to attack 60,000 Federals. Meanwhile, Bragg was assembling 36,000 troops at Versailles to face a single Federal division of 12,000 men.

At least one Confederate commander was beginning to sense a disaster. General Hardee was the author of an authoritative text on military tactics, widely used by both Federals and Confederates. During the night, he

took the time to review copies of Bragg's recent orders, and he was disturbed enough by what he read to take the risk of lecturing his commanding general. "Don't scatter your forces," he implored. "There is one rule in our profession that should never be forgotten — it is to throw the masses of your troops on the fractions of the enemy." Fight at Versailles or fight at Perryville, he said, but in either case, "strike with your whole strength." Hardee added that he thought the first blow ought to be delivered at Perryville, but he was of course unable to back up his opinion with a valid estimate of the size of the Federal force assembling there.

As morning approached, Polk began to realize that he was facing far more Federals than had been previously thought, and he quailed at the idea of launching an attack. During a predawn meeting of Polk and his commanders to discuss what they should do, they learned that Sheridan was driving Liddell's regiments from Doctor's Creek. Now thoroughly alarmed, Polk decided to go on the defensive.

Meanwhile General Bragg had become impatient about the situation at Perryville and decided to take personal command there. He wanted to disperse what he judged to be a small Federal force as rapidly as possible and get his army concentrated farther north. Arriving on the field about 10 a.m., he was distressed to find Polk on the defensive and immediately began shifting troops into assault positions.

Bragg decided to focus his attack against the Federal left. On his right, north of the Mackville Pike, he deployed Cheatham's division plus two brigades from Brigadier General James Patton Anderson's division and one from Major General Simon Bolivar

Major General Benjamin Franklin Cheatham, although distrusted by General Bragg as an incompetent political appointee, led his Tennessee infantry in a disciplined, hard-hitting attack at the Battle of Perryville. "Cheatham's noble division," one officer recalled, "moved forward as if on dress parade."

A 40-year-old Kentucky lawyer who gave up his seat in Congress to join the Federal Army, Brigadier General James S. Jackson commanded the division at Perryville that bore the brunt of the attack by Cheatham's Confederates. Jackson and his two brigade commanders were killed trying to rally their inexperienced troops.

Buckner's. On the far right, Cheatham's line extended along Chaplin River, north of its confluence with Doctor's Creek. The right wing, with Polk in command, was ordered to attack first, at 1 p.m. In the Confederate center, under Hardee, the rest of Buckner's and Anderson's divisions extended the line from the Mackville Pike south to the Springfield Pike. They were to move out immediately after Polk's troops attacked. There had been no activity on the left and Bragg, unaware of the approach of Crittenden's corps, sent only Wheeler's cavalry scouting out along the Lebanon Pike.

While Bragg shifted his forces, his opposite number on the Federal side had to cope with frustration. The previous evening, Buell had ordered McCook and Crittenden to leave their bivouacs promptly at 3 a.m. so as to be in line with Gilbert and ready to attack at 10 a.m. But the message did not reach the generals in time, and they were

late getting under way. When midmorning passed with no sound of a general engagement reaching Buell's headquarters, he assumed that he would have to wait until the next day to attack.

At noon, Cheatham's artillery began to bombard the Federal batteries as a preliminary to the Confederate attack. But the cannonade went on and on, for an hour and a half, with no attack forthcoming. Bragg rode up to Polk and demanded to know why Cheatham's troops had not moved forward on schedule. Polk explained that a Federal column was approaching from the northwest along the Mackville Pike. If he committed his infantry to a frontal assault while the approaching enemy column was still unengaged and able to maneuver, the oncoming Federals might fall on Cheatham's right flank. Therefore, Polk had decided to wait until the column moved into the Federal line. Bragg agreed to the delay, ordered

About 2 p.m. on the afternoon o[f] tober 8, General Braxton B[ragg] launched his initial attack acros[s] shallow Chaplin River north of P[erry]ville with a division under [Gen]eral Benjamin F. Cheatham. [The] Confederates struck General [Alex]ander McCook's corps on the Fe[deral] left and drove it back more t[han a] mile. William Hardee's two Co[nfed]erate divisions under Gen[erals] Buckner and Anderson then atta[cked] the Federal center. The Confede[rates] suffered heavy losses from [the] head-on assaults, and their adv[ance] eventually stalled. Althoug[h his] troops had an edge on the day, B[ragg] realized that he was outnumbere[d and] cautiously ordered a retreat from [Per]ryville during the hours of dark[ness.]

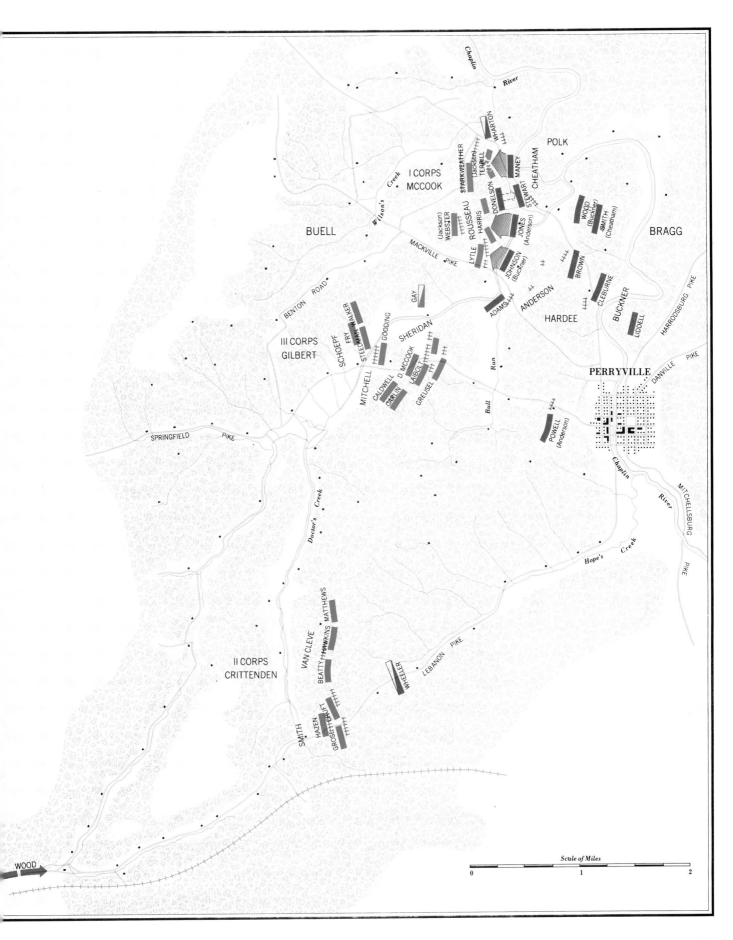

Chaplin River

POLK

I CORPS
McCOOK

BUELL

WHARTON

SPARKWEATHER
TERRILL
(Jackson)
MANEY
CHEATHAM

DONELSON
STEWART

(Jackson)
WEBSTER
ROUSSEAU
HARRIS
LYTLE
JONES
(Anderson)

Wilson's Creek

MACKVILLE PIKE

WOOD
(Buckner)
SMITH
(Cheatham)

BRAGG

JOHNSON
(Buckner)
BROWN
CLEBURNE
BUCKNER
LIDDELL

BENTON ROAD

GAY

ADAMS
ANDERSON
HARDEE

HARRODSBURG PIKE

III CORPS
GILBERT

SCHOEPF
FRY
WALKER
STEEDMAN
GOODING
SHERIDAN

MITCHELL
CALDWELL
CARLIN
D. McCOOK
LAIBOLDT
GREUSEL

Bull Run

PERRYVILLE

DANVILLE PIKE

POWELL
(Anderson)

Chaplin River

MITCHELLSBURG PIKE

SPRINGFIELD PIKE

Doctor's Creek

Hope's Creek

II CORPS
CRITTENDEN

VAN CLEVE
BEATTY
HAWKINS
MATTHEWS

WHEELER

LEBANON PIKE

SMITH
HAZEN
GROSE
CRUFT

WOOD

Scale of Miles

0   1   2

63

Cheatham's line extended farther to the right and rode back to the rear to wait. By now the Confederate guns had ceased firing, and the entire field was silent.

The approaching Federals belonged to McCook's corps, and with their arrival nearly the entire Army of the Ohio was present on the field — Crittenden was quietly taking his place on Gilbert's right during the late morning. But Bragg remained unaware of the odds facing him. As soon as McCook's newcomers began to file into place along the ridge on the north side of the Mackville Pike, before they could settle into place and become familiar with their ground, the Confederates attacked.

General Cheatham rode forward shouting, "Give 'em hell, boys!" General Polk, excited but ever conscious of the fact that he

was also an Episcopal bishop, joined in: "Give it to 'em, boys, give 'em what General Cheatham says!"

The Tennessee brigade leading the Confederate attack charged across the Chaplin River, led by its commander, Brigadier General Daniel Smith Donelson. As the men charged uphill toward the enemy lines, they were caught in a murderous artillery crossfire. An advanced Federal battery of eight 12-pounder Napoleons commanded by Lieutenant Charles C. Parsons blazed away from the ridge, while Captain Samuel J. Harris' 19th Indiana Light Artillery fired from a hill farther to the rear. The shells tore great gaps in the Confederate line, and the onslaught slowed; soon the exhausted survivors sought shelter in a small wood and waited for help to arrive.

At a critical moment in the Perryvil battle, about 3:30 in the afternoon, the 19th Indiana Battery (right) and the 80th Indiana Infantry (foregrou manage to withstand a fierce charg by the 31st Tennessee (background left). The Confederates, a Federal ficer recalled, attacked "with deatt defying steadiness, uttering wild ye until staggered by the sweeping cro fire of our artillery and the volleys from Starkweather's regiments."

Meanwhile, Cheatham's other brigades were advancing, A. P. Stewart's behind Donelson's and General Thomas Jones's untried Mississippians to the left. Seeing Donelson's plight, Cheatham ordered Brigadier General George Earl Maney's Tennessee brigade to go to his support.

As one of Maney's regiments, the 27th Tennessee, moved up, two young soldiers approached Captain John W. Carroll to say that they knew they were about to be killed. "Their pale features, their calm demeanor, their determined looks impressed me much," Carroll recalled. "While I had no authority to offer such a thing, yet I did offer that they take a pass and drop out, which they refused to do." Both were killed.

The Tennessee brigade made it as far as the woods, but there it, too, was halted by the artillery fire. Maney moved among the trees, rallying his men as Federal shells sent branches crashing down and lethal splinters flying. He somehow managed to mount another charge; his men roared out of the woods, overran Parsons' battery and continued up the slope. They reached the top and caught the Federals off balance — fresh troops had just arrived, and there was confusion as they took their places in the line.

Cheatham's Confederates dealt the poorly deployed Federals a smashing blow, the fire of Maney's regiments looking, a Confederate combatant recalled, "as if it were a solid sheet of flame." According to one Federal officer facing the attack, the bullets "sounded like a swarm of bees running away in the hot summer air overhead." The Federal division commander, Brigadier General James S. Jackson, went down mortally wounded. Brigadier General William Terrill struggled to hold the line with his green brigade, but the men were driven back in savage, hand-to-hand fighting. Cheatham's men were soon supported by cannon that had been hauled laboriously over the steep bluffs of the Chaplin River. At length, Terrill's decimated lines broke, and his men rushed toward the rear.

They tried to make a stand about a mile to the west, but their ranks were broken again by Stewart's and Donelson's onrushing brigades. Major James A. Connolly, seeing General Terrill struck down by an artillery shell, rushed to his fallen commander. "I raised him to a sitting position and saw that nearly his entire breast was torn away by the shell," Connolly wrote later. "He recognized me and his first words were: 'Major, do you think it is fatal?' I knew it must be, but to encourage him I answered, 'Oh

I hope not, General.' He then said, 'My poor wife, my poor wife.' He lived until 2 o'clock next morning.''

When the Confederates had cut their way almost completely through McCook's corps, they ran into a brigade under the command of Brigadier General John C. Starkweather. Grimly, Starkweather's veterans breasted the onslaught and after desperate fighting, they stopped Donelson's brigade and began to drive it back.

McCook asked Sheridan to send help, but Sheridan was under attack by two of Anderson's brigades. And to the north of Sheridan's position, between the Springfield and Mackville Pikes, others of Hardee's Confederate troops had found a gap between Gilbert's left and McCook's right, and they were plunging into the opening.

General Gilbert ordered his batteries to fire obliquely at the advancing Confederates and sent two of his brigades under Colonel Michael Gooding and Brigadier General James B. Steedman to block the Confederate assault. Gilbert's troops were steadily driven back. Gooding recalled: "The battle now raged furiously; one after one my men were cut down." But finally the advance slowed in the face of the fierce opposition; then, in the growing darkness, it stopped.

Remarkably, General Buell did not know until 4 p.m. that his army was engaged in a furious battle. Atmospheric conditions were such that the roar of the guns could not be heard at Buell's headquarters only a few miles from the front. Consequently, Buell arrived too late to do anything but oversee General Gilbert's deployments and send one brigade from Gilbert to assist McCook.

Crittenden's entire corps, meanwhile, remained stationary a few miles down the Lebanon Pike. This corps could have turned the Confederate left and changed the course of the battle, but Crittenden was thoroughly intimidated by Wheeler's small cavalry force; Crittenden lacked both initiative and orders, and his corps sat out the battle.

By contrast, the aggressive Sheridan managed late in the afternoon to go on the offensive despite heavy casualties. He drove Anderson's brigades back toward Perryville, and a brigade under Colonel William Carlin, moving up in support of Sheridan's men, actually charged into the streets of the town. A staff officer sent by Gilbert remembered the exultant Sheridan saying that "he had driven the enemy before him, and whipped them like hell." But once again Sheridan was getting too far out in front; McCook's broken and disorganized corps had been pounded back more than a mile. Fearing a counterattack, Sheridan and Carlin halted and consolidated their positions just west of the town.

As night fell, the Confederates held advanced positions, but their lines were so irregular that units on both sides became confused in the gathering darkness. General Polk ran afoul of the confusion. In the twilight he saw what he thought was a body of Confederates firing, apparently by mistake, on a regiment of comrades. Riding up to the colonel commanding the offending unit, Polk ordered him to cease firing on friendly soldiers. The colonel replied that he was sure that his troops were firing on the enemy.

Polk disagreed, and he roared, "Cease firing, sir; what is your name, sir?"

The colonel gave his name, identified his unit as an Indiana regiment and asked Polk: "Pray, sir, who are you?"

Stunned by the realization that he had ridden into the midst of a Federal regiment,

Brigadier General Sterling Alexand Martin Wood — known as Sam fro his initials — was badly wounded I a shell fragment while leading his b gade of Buckner's division against Federal center at Perryville. Wood recovered from his wound but resigned his commission about a year later, apparently angry that his leadership in subsequent battles had no been noted in official reports.

Polk could only rely on the concealing darkness — and bluster. "I'll soon show you who I am," he growled. "Cease firing at once!"

Then, flinching in anticipation of a volley that never came, he turned his horse and cantered unscathed back to his lines.

Skirmishing continued after dark, but the battle was over. The Federals had suffered the higher casualties — 845 dead, 2,851 wounded and 515 missing. The Confederate toll was 3,396. Clearly, Bragg was the victor of this day's action.

The moon was bright and almost full that night, and many of the Federal officers who met at Buell's headquarters after the battle urged another attack in the moonlight. But Buell, convinced that he faced Bragg's entire army, decided to wait until morning. By then it was too late.

That night General Bragg finally understood that he had been fighting the whole Army of the Ohio. And it dawned on him in the midst of victory that although his Confederate troops had fought gallantly and well, they had survived the precarious situation only because of Federal blunders. After consulting with Hardee and Polk, Bragg ordered an immediate and hasty retreat to Harrodsburg, where he could yet again concentrate his forces and counter any move by Buell to cut the Confederate line of retreat to Tennessee. In the end, no one gained at the Battle of Perryville.

Private Sam Watkins of the 1st Tennessee put a proper epitaph upon the sorry struggle: "If it had been two men wrestling it could have been called a 'dog fall.' Both sides claiming the victory — both whipped."

Nashville under Federal Rule

To the strains of "Yankee Doodle," Federal troops marched into Nashville's nearly deserted streets on February 24, 1862, taking possession of the first Confederate state capital to fall to the Union. Nashvillians could only suffer in silence as the Federals made themselves at home, commandeering buildings, cutting down fine old trees for firewood and threatening to jail leading citizens unless they signed humiliating oaths of allegiance to the Union. Proper young ladies spurned even the most courteous Federal officers, scorning them with what one girl called "looks of silent malediction."

The sedate city of 17,000 was soon transformed into a wartime boom town. The Federals imported droves of workers to operate storage, shipping and medical facilities. Escaped slaves sought refuge in the occupied city. The lure of easy money drew a host of unsavory characters who hoped to profit from the city's war-fueled economy. At length Nashville's population swelled to 80,000; a wave of crime and drunkenness swept the city, threatening for a time a complete breakdown of law and order.

Yet the city survived, and the occupation even had some lighter moments. The Nashville Theater remained open, offering such classics as Shakespeare's *Hamlet*. Once during that play's graveyard scene, when the hero found the skull of Yorick, a soldier jeered from the back of the theater, "Hey pard, what is it — Yank or Reb?" The audience dissolved in laughter, and the tensions, for a moment, were broken among war-weary people.

Steamboats lie moored to Nashville's wharf in December 1862 as stevedores unload hardtack, flour, sugar, molasses and whiskey. Nashville afforded ready access to the Mississippi, Ohio and Tennessee Rivers, and became a strategic supply center for Federal armies in the West.

With the cupola of the State Capitol dominating the skyline, and the Cumberland flowing peacefully *(top right)*, wartime Nashville betrays few outward signs of the privations endured by its inhabitants. Housing was scarce and crowded, fuel for heating often unavailable and fresh food supplies cut off by Confederate raids. The city, lamented Nashville's *Daily Press,* was "filled with thugs, highwaymen, robbers and assassins."

A stately home on High Street, one of hundreds commandeered by Federal forces, served as headquarters for General William S. Rosecrans, commander of the 50,000-man Army of the Cumberland.

As curious civilians look on, Federal troops stand in formation outside Nashville's unfinished Maxwell House Hotel, which provided quarters for troops in transit.

The State Capitol, surrounded by the tents and shelters of Union troops, anchored a line of forts and strongpoints that girdled Nashville's southern approaches. Local slaveowners reluctantly supplied the labor and material for the defenses under orders from Andrew Johnson, the military governor of the state, who decreed that "rebels must be made to feel the burden of their deeds."

Fortified right up to its towering portico, the Capitol is protected by earthworks and a sturdy stockade made from trees felled in city parks. These defenses, backed up by 15 heavy cannon and several companies of infantry bivouacked in the Statehouse, provided reassurance to the Union occupiers in 1862, when the demands of war elsewhere left only 2,000 men defending the city.

Nashville's Howard School, pressed into service as a 250-bed hospital, was one of 25 Federal medical facilities in the capital.

The U.S. Sanitary Commission turned the Planters Hotel into a center for convalescent officers.

In the yard of Nashville's Union Hospital No. 19, volunteers and former slaves hang out the bed linens and hospital gowns at laundry time.

Sentry boxes and massive wooden gates guard Nashville's railroad bridge across the Cumberland River. Although retreating Confederates wrecked the city's bridges, Union engineers quickly repaired this span, replacing the rails and laying down heavy planking to permit horse-drawn traffic as well as trains.

Taylor Depot, a massive warehouse at the terminal of the Nashville & Chattanooga Railroad, held as many as 15 million complete rations — a day's provisions for one soldier — for the Union Army's Commissary Department. During one 10-month period, the city's warehouses shipped 200,000 blankets, 450,000 pairs of shoes and 500,000 tents to Union troops in the field.

Locomotives stand ready for service in Nashville's busy railroad depot. Under the control of Union logistics experts, with headquarters in the building at far

essee's railroads became models of military efficiency, carrying men and supplies to the front while shuttling prisoners and the sick and wounded to the rear.

Clash at Doctor's Creek

"The President is greatly dissatisfied with your delay, and has sent for me several times to account for it. He has repeated to me time and again that there were imperative reasons why the enemy should be driven across the Tennessee River at the earliest possible moment."

MAJOR GENERAL HENRY W. HALLECK TO MAJOR GENERAL WILLIAM S. ROSECRANS, DECEMBER 5, 1862

3

The sting of his near removal had propelled General Don Carlos Buell into battle, but it did not provide him with sufficient drive to defeat Bragg. To the despair of President Lincoln, Buell failed to press the issue after Perryville despite his considerable advantages. Given a chance to pursue Bragg's outnumbered and retreating army out of Tennessee, Buell refused.

On October 16, Buell informed Washington that he would not follow the Confederates because the roads were too rough and the country too barren. As he had argued during the summer, Buell now insisted that the preferable route into eastern Tennessee was from the south, not the north. He would reassemble the army in Nashville, return to northern Alabama and attack Chattanooga from there.

The response from General in Chief Halleck was sharp: Buell should not retire but instead should "drive the enemy from Kentucky and East Tennessee. If we cannot do it now, we need never to hope for it." The President, Halleck wrote in a later message, "does not understand why we cannot march as the enemy marches, live as he lives, and fight as he fights, unless we admit the inferiority of our troops and of our generals."

Buell readily admitted exactly that. "The spirit of the rebellion," he complained in a long account of his problems on October 22, "enforces a subordination and patient submission to privation and want which public sentiment renders absolutely impossible among our troops." Because of this fortitude, plus a willingness among the Confederates to impose the death penalty, "the discipline of the rebel army is superior to ours."

Lincoln obviously thought that the inferiority resided not in the troops but in their general. On October 23, he relieved Buell and replaced him with Major General William S. Rosecrans. The Union had retained Kentucky by default, but the problem of East Tennessee remained, and the Administration wanted it solved. Halleck's letter of instructions to Rosecrans about his new duties ended with a stern warning: "Neither the country nor the Government will much longer put up with the inactivity of some of our armies and generals."

Rosecrans had enjoyed a modestly successful wartime career. Early in 1861, he had joined General George B. McClellan's Department of the Ohio as a colonel of engineers. Serving in western Virginia, he rose rapidly in rank and assumed command of the Federal forces there when McClellan was called to Washington. Sent later to join Grant in Tennessee, Rosecrans had driven Sterling Price from Iuka in September and defeated Earl Van Dorn at Corinth in October, in both cases after heavy fighting. By that time, Buell's timidity had become painfully obvious, and Rosecrans appeared to Lincoln to be one of the few real fighters among the Federal generals.

The burly, six-foot-tall Rosecrans —

dubbed Old Rosy by his troops — was 43 years old when he took command of what was now designated the Army of the Cumberland. He had blond hair, a close-cropped beard and a large, hooked, red nose described by a contemporary as "an intensified Roman nose" in a sly reference to Rosecrans' hard drinking. Quick to anger, the general was just as quick to forgive. He would berate an officer terribly and then restore the man to good humor with moderating gestures and smiles. Rosecrans was a passionate convert to Roman Catholicism and often engaged his staff in nocturnal religious discussions, in one period keeping them up until 4 a.m. for 10 nights in a row.

Rosecrans' soldiers, in the manner of the times, expressed their enthusiasm for his promotion by bellowing an artless song: "Old Rosy is our man, Old Rosy is our man. He'll show his deeds where'er he leads. Old Rosy is our man." But their good will could

not change the fact that the men, having marched more than 700 miles, had outdistanced their supplies. The problems that had undone Buell remained to be solved.

Buell had already started the army toward Nashville, and Rosecrans did not change those orders. But the relocation to Nashville did not end the Federal supply difficulties, in spite of the fact that the city was located on the Cumberland River and served by the railroad from Louisville. The river was still too low for navigation, and the railroad was still being torn up regularly by Confederate cavalry raids.

At Nashville, Rosecrans went to work. Relying heavily on wagons, Rosecrans restocked his supplies and reequipped his army. He rested his veterans and trained his recruits — while keeping a wary eye on the Confederates.

He also had to deal with problems of civil law and order. The army's provost marshal, John Fitch, complained that "Nashville was a rebel city, swarming with traitors, smugglers and spies. Of its male inhabitants, a large number were in the rebel army; and its women, arrogant and defiant, were alike, outspoken in their treason and indefatigable in their efforts to aid that cause for which their brothers, sons and husbands were fighting." Rosecrans organized a secret service and a police department, ferreted out the smugglers and spies, seized contraband and imprisoned the culprits or expelled them from the Federal lines.

Rosecrans used his imagination to solve another problem. Many Federal soldiers were deliberately surrendering to the Confederates, knowing that they might be paroled and sent home. This practice, Fitch reported, was greatly reduced by an order from Rosecrans "directing that all thus practically guilty of desertion should have their heads encased in white cotton night caps and thus publicly branded as cowards, be marched through the streets and camps and sent North."

All this took time, during which Halleck and Lincoln repeatedly prodded their new general for action. On December 4, Halleck applied the lash: "The President is very impatient at your long stay in Nashville. The favorable season for your campaign will soon be over. You give Bragg time to supply himself by plundering the country your army should have occupied. Twice have I been asked to designate someone else to command your army. If you remain one more week at Nashville, I cannot prevent your removal."

But Rosecrans refused to budge until his army was ready. "I need no other stimulus to make me do my duty than the knowledge of what it is," he replied. "To threats of removal or the like I must be permitted to say that I am insensible."

On October 23, the day Buell was relieved, General Braxton Bragg had received a peremptory summons from his old friend, President Jefferson Davis. The telegram read: "The President desires that you will lose no time in coming here."

Bragg had just reached Knoxville after the long retreat from Kentucky. It had been a dismal 200-mile journey over rough and muddy roads. Many of the troops had no shoes, and their clothing hung in shreds. Along the way they found little to eat; parched corn was all that kept many from starvation. More than 15,000 troops were struck down during the march by typhoid, scurvy, dysentery and pneumonia.

The rigors of the retreat made Bragg's Kentucky invasion seem all the more pointless and wasteful. Now his principal subordinates were almost in open revolt, his men were bitter and disheartened, and there was a growing public outcry across the Confederacy for his removal. "General Bragg is either stark mad or utterly incompetent," wrote a surgeon who had been on the staff of General Albert Sidney Johnston. A Kentuckian believed "Bragg to be both sane and loyal, but I concur in the judgment that he is utterly incompetent." The diarist Mary Chesnut, writing in Richmond, observed that Bragg had "a winning way of earning everybody's detestation."

Jefferson Davis was not one to yield hastily to public opinion. He blamed much of the furor on his political enemies, alleging that they really were attacking him through his well-known friendship with Bragg. Davis was deeply concerned, however, by the criticism from Bragg's officers and men. Generals Polk, Kirby Smith and Hardee had all been vociferous in their condemnation of Bragg's leadership. Brigadier General Henry Heth wrote that he and Kirby Smith "came to the conclusion that General Bragg had lost his mind." Tennessee Senator Gustavus Adolphus Henry, who was in Knoxville when the Confederates straggled into town, observed the discontent of Bragg's men. He reported: "Never have I heard so much dissatisfaction as the army expresses at the result of General Bragg's campaign. The army is clamoring for Joe Johnston to lead them, or for Beauregard. The safety of the army depends upon a change of commanders."

Where Buell had blamed his reverses on lack of discipline, Bragg the disciplinarian railed against the citizens of Kentucky. In a

General William Rosecrans br
new spirit to the Army of the Cu
land after its lackluster perform
at the Battle of Perryville
general was, wrote one of his sta
man from whom the people are
day expecting some extraordina
tion, some tremendous ba

bitter letter to his wife, Bragg wondered, "Why should I stay with my handful of brave Southern men to fight for cowards who skulked about in the dark to say to us, 'We are with you. Only whip these fellows out of our country and let us see you can protect us, and we will join you.' "

But Bragg was apparently somewhat abashed by the uproar, and for once he was not contentious in his meeting with the President. Instead he adopted a straightforward, modest manner. He told Davis that the retreat from Kentucky had been necessary to save his starving army.

And in fact, Bragg had something to show for his efforts. He had inflicted 25,000 Federal casualties, and he had captured ammunition and more than 30 pieces of artillery and hundreds of wagons, horses, mules and guns. The army was intact, albeit half its original size. Moreover, in the aftermath of the Confederate defeats at Iuka and Corinth, Bragg's was the only force in the field able to resist a Federal drive into the Deep South.

Along with his explanation, Bragg offered President Davis a new plan of operations: Bragg would move his army to Murfreesboro and from there attack Nashville. Eventually, Davis pronounced himself satisfied, sent Bragg back to Tennessee to resume his command and moved quickly to neutralize Bragg's rebellious generals. He called Leonidas Polk and Kirby Smith to Richmond, heard them out, placated each of them with the third star of a lieutenant general and persuaded them to return to their duties. Davis had in mind one more remedy for the dissension in the west, but for the time being he kept it to himself.

Bragg had sent General Breckinridge to take command at Murfreesboro. He arrived

there with his 6,000-man division on October 28 under Bragg's typically vague instructions to prepare "for the defense of Middle Tennessee or an attack on Nashville."

While Breckinridge waited for the main army to arrive, he fretted that the Federals would learn how small his force was and drive him south. As a show of strength, he ordered a new series of cavalry raids by Forrest and Morgan. On November 6, Morgan attacked toward Nashville from the north, while Forrest attacked from the south. Both cavalry forces skirmished vigorously with Federal troops but with few significant results. Forrest said afterward that he believed the Confederates could have taken Nashville at any time and should have. But it was too late: Rosecrans and the Army of the Cumberland marched in on November 7.

Bragg's army, meanwhile, was suffering

cruelly from exposure and disease. More than 15,000 troops filled hospitals from eastern Tennessee to northern Georgia. With six inches of snow on the ground in eastern Tennessee by November 1, the remaining 27,000 troops lacked clothing, equipment and shelter to protect them from the bitter weather.

They were also short of food, although plenty of provisions were stockpiled in the area. The Confederate government had decreed that supplies in eastern Tennessee were to be reserved for the exclusive use of the Army of Northern Virginia, whose campaign in the East was considered to be more important. While Bragg's men were foraging desperately across the countryside, nearby warehouses were shipping eastward thousands of cattle and hogs, barrels of flour, bushels of wheat and sides of bacon.

Around the 1st of November, Bragg's

Designed by Adolphus Heiman, a Prussian immigrant, and opened i the early 1850s, the suspension br over the Cumberland River at Nas ville was one of the city's landmar Retreating Confederates cut its ca bles in February 1862, leaving onl the abutments standing.

troops were moved to Chattanooga, then to Tullahoma and finally through the Stones River valley toward Murfreesboro. Even though the valley had been foraged by Buell's Federals during the summer, it still offered some sustenance. And when the advance elements began to arrive in Murfreesboro on the 20th of November, they discovered that Bragg had managed to gather an ample supply of food. Slowly, the men began to recover from their ordeal.

On November 24, President Davis unveiled his solution for the vexing problem of coordinating the Confederate forces in Tennessee and Mississippi: He assigned General Joseph E. Johnston to overall command of the Western Theater. In Davis' view, Richmond was too far away to decide the issues of troop allocation and campaign objectives that continually arose among the armies and departments. Davis placed Kirby Smith's forces under Bragg's jurisdiction and renamed Bragg's army the Army of Tennessee. He wanted Johnston to oversee the operations of both Bragg's forces and Lieutenant General John C. Pemberton's army at Vicksburg in Mississippi. Almost immediately, the new arrangement generated more difficulties than it solved.

Johnston and Davis had been at loggerheads since the beginning of the War. Indeed, some traced their acrimonious relationship to a fistfight the two men had had over a girl while they both were West Point cadets. But their wartime disagreements started when Johnston, who had been the Quartermaster General of the United States Army in 1860 and thought of himself as the senior Confederate general when the War broke out, was instead ranked fourth in seniority by Davis. Despite Johnston's injured

pride, he fought well at First Bull Run and was wounded at Seven Pines in June of 1862. The command in the west was the first assignment following his recovery.

Johnston saw at once that his task was impossible. While Rosecrans was gathering his resources to move against Bragg, Grant was preparing to advance on Pemberton at Vicksburg; the two Confederate armies were isolated from each other, undersupplied and undermanned. Before leaving Richmond to establish headquarters at Chattanooga, Johnston proposed that Pemberton's army be brought to central Tennessee and combined with Bragg's army to drive Rosecrans from the state, thus forcing Grant to abandon his advance into Mississippi.

Davis not only brushed aside Johnston's suggestion but a few days later proposed strongly that Johnston send some of Bragg's men to reinforce Pemberton. Instead of complying, Johnston pointed out, as he had before, that Vicksburg could be reinforced more sensibly by a 30,000-man army that was presently in Arkansas, doing nothing. Bragg could not deplete his army further, Johnston said, "without exposing himself to inevitable defeat."

The Confederates had one thing to cheer about, however, as a consequence of John Hunt Morgan's splendidly combative nature. Assigned by Bragg to harass the Federal supply lines to Nashville, Morgan immediately set his sights on the railroad from Louisville. But he would have to contend with a Federal brigade at Hartsville, 35 miles northeast of Nashville, that was in an admirable position to defend the railroad line.

On December 6, while Confederate infantry units feinted toward Lavergne on the Nashville-Murfreesboro road and against

In one of many skirmishes between units of the maneuvering armies after the Battle of Perryville, the 31st Ohio, foreground and at right, repulses an attack by John Hunt Morgan's cavalry. The Federals are defending Cage's Ford on the Cumberland River near Gallatin, Tennessee.

Lebanon, northeast of Nashville, Morgan's raiders set out for Hartsville. The force comprised four regiments of mixed infantry and one battalion of cavalry under Colonel Basil Duke, and two regiments of Kentucky infantry commanded by Colonel Thomas H. Hunt, Morgan's uncle. In bitter cold, they rode and marched across snow-covered ground toward Hartsville; to get there, they would have to cross the icy Cumberland River just below their objective.

To move rapidly without becoming exhausted, the infantry and cavalry took turns riding the available horses. "This was an injudicious measure," Colonel Duke wrote later. "The infantry had gotten their feet wet in trudging through the snow, and after riding a short time, were nearly frozen and clamored to dismount. The cavalrymen had now gotten their feet saturated with moisture, and when they remounted, suffered greatly in their turn. There was some trouble, too, in returning the horses to the proper parties after dark, and the infantrymen damned the cavalry service with all the resources of a soldier's vocabulary."

Crossing the Cumberland that night proved even more difficult than expected. Morgan took the infantry to a ferry crossing, while Duke led the cavalry to a ford some miles downstream. The infantrymen found only two boats, and it took most of the night for the troops to be relayed across. The horsemen fared worse. "The men could reach the river bank only by a narrow bridle path which admitted only one man at a time. They were then compelled to gather their horses and leap into the river, over the bluff about four feet high. Horse and rider would generally be submerged by the plunge. The cold after the ducking affected the men hor-

87

ribly; those who got across first built fires, at which they partially warmed themselves while the others were crossing."

When it became apparent that the whole force would not get over the river by daylight, Duke took the troopers who had made it across and set out to meet Morgan at a rendezvous three miles from the Federal encampment at Hartsville. On the way, the cavalrymen ran into some Federal pickets and drove them back, thus losing the element of surprise. Forewarned, the Federals were able to deploy in battle lines in front of their encampment.

As Duke rode up to the meeting place, Morgan informed him that there were 1,000 more Federals in Hartsville than they had thought. Duke recalled saying to Morgan: "You have more work cut out for you than you bargained for."

Duke dismounted his cavalry and hit the Federal right, driving it back. While this attack was under way, two Confederate howitzers on the south bank of the Cumberland began peppering the Federal camp, drawing the Federal artillery's fire away from the cavalry attack. Meanwhile, Hunt struck the Federals' left flank with the 2nd Kentucky and then with the 9th Kentucky in echelon.

In short order, Duke wrote, "the enemy were crowded together like sheep in a pen, and were falling fast. The white flag was hoisted in an hour and a half after the first shot had been fired." The Federal commander, Colonel Absalom B. Moore, surrendered his 1,834 troops with all their artillery, equipment and supplies. Morgan's men destroyed the booty and then marched to Murfreesboro with their prisoners.

The little victory at Hartsville delighted President Jefferson Davis, but he found oth-

er things to complain about. Davis remained exasperated by Johnston's opposition to the reinforcement of Pemberton at Vicksburg, and Davis arrived in Murfreesboro on December 10 to inspect Bragg's army for himself. Nothing he saw changed his mind. He ordered Johnston to send Major General Carter Stevenson's division of about 9,000 men — one fourth of Bragg's infantry — to Vicksburg. Bragg protested that he would then have fewer than 40,000 men to oppose Rosecrans, whose force had been estimated at 65,000 in Nashville and another 35,000 guarding his line of communication with Louisville. Bragg also pointed out that he had detached Forrest to raid Grant's supply lines in western Tennessee.

Davis was unyielding. He told Bragg, "Fight if you can and fall back beyond the Tennessee."

The President spent two days in Murfrees-

Samuel Dodd Morgan was one of Nashville's leading merchants and the uncle of the Confederate cavalry leader John Hunt Morgan. Intent on turning Nashville into an arsenal for the Confederacy, Samu[el] Morgan constructed a percussion-cap factory and was instrumental in the establishment of gun foundries and powder mills.

The sprawling T. M. Brennan foundry on Nashville's Front Street began producing ordnance in May 1861.

Brennan's 12-pounder cast-iron field howitzer was distinguished by its bulbous breech. It sold for $350.

Cannon Makers for the Confederacy

Until its occupation by Federal troops in late February of 1862, Nashville served as the armorer of the western Confederacy. Prominent among the city's foundries was T. M. Brennan and Company, which converted from the manufacture of steam engines and farm machinery to the production of fieldpieces. Like many Confederate foundries, the company was forced to improvise. On the basis of information obtained from two Confederate spies who had infiltrated the Fort Pitt foundry in Pittsburgh, Brennan was able to construct his own rifling machine. At peak production, the firm turned out 12 fieldpieces a week — along with carriages, caissons and tons of shot and shell. When Nashville fell, Brennan employees managed to smuggle out the firm's precious rifling machine. The Brennan firm itself was put up for auction by the invading Federals, and the remaining guns were spiked.

boro. Between meetings with the commanders, he inspected the army, was serenaded by the soldiers and addressed a crowd gathered in front of his hotel. In the spirit of the Christmas season, which the people in Murfreesboro were beginning to celebrate early in the President's honor, Davis rewarded Morgan for the Hartsville raid with a commission as a brigadier general. General Hardee urged the President to make Morgan a major general, but Davis replied, "I do not wish to give my boys all their sugar plums at once."

Davis left for Chattanooga on December 13. By then, Murfreesboro was buzzing over another social event — the impending wedding of John Morgan to Mattie Ready, reputed to be the prettiest girl in town.

Mattie Ready, at the age of 17, had caught the attention of the 37-year-old Confederate hero with an outlandishly dramatic gesture. That summer, while Murfreesboro was temporarily occupied by Federal troops, she heard some Yankee officers disparaging the flamboyant Morgan. She defended her hero so staunchly that one of the officers demanded to know her name. "It's Mattie Ready now," she replied, "but by the grace of God one day I hope to call myself the wife of John Morgan." As soon as Morgan returned to Murfreesboro, he heard the story and called on her; he found her to be "as pretty as she was patriotic," and her wish was soon granted.

The wedding ceremony became the event of the Christmas season. The service was performed by General Leonidas Polk, who was also a bishop in the Episcopal Church; and it was attended by all the luminaries of the Army of Tennessee. Then came kindred festivities — parties, horse races and extravagant dinners. All the while, the army was

As part of the campaign against Rosecrans' lines of communication around Nashville, Confederate guerrillas wearing Federal overcoats burn five steamboats on the Cumberland River in early December 1862. The wounded lying on the riverbank were removed from the makeshift sick bay of one of the boats, a passenger recalled, after the guerrillas threatened to burn them along with the vessel.

being fed and feted by wives, fiancées, mothers and relatives, who brought with them not only hampers of delicacies but new clothing and uniforms. These solicitous ministrations were much appreciated but soon contributed to something of a crisis.

Discipline flagged, and drunkenness increased alarmingly. A newspaper editor charged: "A large number of the officers of our Southern Army are hard drinkers, where they are not drunkards." According to an apocryphal story that went the rounds, a young recruit was given a dollar and told to go buy food and drink from the sutler. He returned with 90 cents' worth of whiskey and 10 cents' worth of food. He was berated for wasting so much money on food.

Still, picket duty, guard duty and drill occupied much of the soldiers' time. They also kept busy constructing crude huts and houses around Murfreesboro in case they

had to spend the dead of winter in place. There were small, sporadic actions. A week after his wedding, Morgan kissed his bride good-by and set out on a two-week raid into Kentucky, during which he destroyed miles of Louisville & Nashville Railroad track, took nearly 2,000 prisoners and destroyed two million dollars' worth of property.

Bragg spent the Christmas season waiting for Rosecrans' next move. The Army of Tennessee was aligned in a 32-mile-long crescent centered on Murfreesboro and facing Nashville. General Hardee commanded the left wing, based in Triune, a village 14 miles west of Murfreesboro on the McClensville Pike leading south from Nashville; the center, under General Polk, was at Murfreesboro, where Bragg had his headquarters; the right was located at Readyville, 12 miles east of Murfreesboro, and was held by General McCown's division of Hardee's corps.

Bragg had reorganized his cavalry, detach-
ing the units under Morgan and Forrest for
"special service" and placing the remaining horsemen under the command of 26-
year-old Joseph Wheeler. The young man
had been out of West Point for only three
years and had been a brigadier general for
two months, but he had already earned the
nickname Fighting Joe. Wheeler's troopers
continually patrolled the countryside between Bragg's line and Nashville, watch-
ing for Rosecrans.

For the Federal troops, it was a lonely, de-
pressing Christmas. Some soldiers in the
74th Ohio augmented their diet by hunting
robins in a canebrake at night. "With a torch
in one hand and a stick in the other we knock
them off the bushes," one of the soldiers

wrote. "Night before last we killed 30, and
last night 26. We had some flour yesterday,
and we made a pot pie for dinner."

Colonel John Beatty had a more traditional Christmas dinner. "At an expense of one
dollar and seventy-five cents," he wrote, "I
procured a small turkey; but it lacked the
collaterals, and was a failure." He was nonetheless thankful: "For 20 months now I have
been a sojourner in camps, a dweller in tents,
going hither and yon, at all hours of the day
and night, in all sorts of weather, sleeping for
weeks at a stretch without shelter, and yet I
have been strong and healthy."

On Christmas Day, General Rosecrans
was ready for battle at last. He issued orders
for the Army of the Cumberland to advance
on Murfreesboro the next day. At a war
council on Christmas night, Rosecrans told
his generals that the Confederates were now
more vulnerable than ever: He had learned
that Bragg had lost the services of Stevenson's division and had sent Forrest and Morgan away on raids.

Rosecrans went over his plans with the
generals, and after a while he put a sudden end to the discussion that followed by
banging a mug of toddy on a table and
springing to his feet. "We move tomorrow,
gentlemen! We shall begin to skirmish,
probably as soon as we pass the outposts.
Press them hard! Drive them out of their
nests! Make them fight or run! Fight them!
Fight them! Fight, I say!"

Heavy rain, typical of winter in Tennessee,
began to fall that night. In the cold, gray
dawn, three columns of Federal troops
trudged out of Nashville by separate routes.
General Crittenden, on the Federal left, took
three divisions down the Nashville Pike.

the armies converged on Murboro, the place was described by server as a handsome and aristic town where "the poor whites s poor as rot, and the rich are ich." In the views above, the y house, scene of John Hunt an's marriage, is flanked by the ler mansion on the left and the house on the right.

McCook, with three infantry divisions and Stanley's cavalry brigade, marched in the center down the Nolensville Pike toward Triune, where he was to turn eastward toward Murfreesboro. George Thomas, on the right, was to take the Franklin Turnpike south from Nashville to Brentwood, then turn east, cross in the rear of McCook at Nolensville and continue on to Murfreesboro. Thomas had one division and three brigades with him — less than half of his command. Indeed, little more than half of the Army of the Cumberland — 44,000 of the 82,000 men available — actually took part in the advance. The rest remained in garrison in Nashville and guarded the railroad to Louisville.

Just as Rosecrans had predicted, the advancing columns ran into Confederate cavalry units soon after passing the outposts of Nashville. First contact was made by

McCook's wing, which at 7 a.m. attacked a detachment at Nolensville. The Confederate cavalry there, commanded by Brigadier General John A. Wharton, withdrew toward the south in good order and formed a line on the ridges north of Triune. There Wharton's artillery commenced a duel with McCook's. On hearing the firing, General Thomas turned eastward to march to McCook's assistance.

At about the same time, Crittenden, to the northeast, ran into Wheeler's outposts, deployed north of Lavergne on the Nashville-Murfreesboro road. Later that day, as Crittenden pushed on closer to Lavergne, he encountered stiff resistance from Wheeler's entire brigade, reinforced by George Maney's brigade of Tennesseans. A pattern was emerging in which the Federals, instead of making a rapid advance on the main Confederate army, were continually being forced to stop, form a line of battle and clear their path of stubborn, well-deployed cavalry units.

With the time gained by the cavalry's successful delaying tactics, Bragg began to consolidate his army. He called McCown in from Readyville and Hardee from the Triune area. Wharton hung on stubbornly at Triune until the superior Federal artillery drove him out of his line. By nightfall on December 27, Wharton and his infantry support had withdrawn to Murfreesboro.

Unsure in the face of the three-pronged advance where the main Federal effort would be made, Bragg threw a defensive line across all the approaches to Murfreesboro from the northwest. Polk was placed more than a mile west of the town, where the Stones River curved behind his back, while Hardee was an equal distance out to the northwest, across the river from Polk.

It was a terrible position for any kind of fighting. Hardee wrote later that "the field of battle offered no peculiar advantages for defense. The country on every side was open and accessible to the enemy." It was rough ground, interspersed with limestone shelves, large boulders and deep crevices, and dotted with thick stands of red cedar.

Polk faced his troops to the west in a semicircle across the Franklin road, the Wilkinson Pike and the Nashville Pike. General Jones Withers' division was placed in the front line, with Cheatham's division in reserve along the banks of the river. Private Sam Watkins of Company H, Cheatham's 1st Tennessee, wrote later that the line of battle was formed on the wrong side of Stones River — "on the Yankee side. Bad generalship, I thought."

Hardee's corps extended from the east

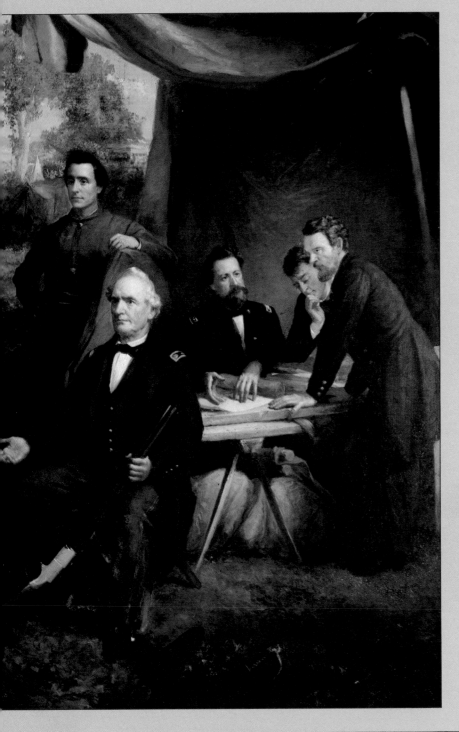

A Clan Called to Arms for the Union

Marching with Rosecrans in the Army of the Cumberland were four general officers by the name of McCook. They were members of a formidable Ohio family that sent so many men to fight for the Union — 15 in all — that the clan became known as "the Fighting McCooks." The oldest in service was lawyer Daniel McCook, who volunteered at 63 and died in the War along with three of eight sons who served. Also in the War was Daniel's brother John, who enlisted with his five sons.

All 15 McCooks were markedly brave, and some distinguished themselves. Brigadier General Edward Moody McCook commanded a cavalry division in the Army of the Cumberland and with his brother Anson took part in Sherman's march through Georgia. Brigadier General Daniel McCook Jr. recited to his men a passage from Macaulay's poem "Horatius" — "And how can man die better / Than facing fearful odds?" — before leading an assault on Confederate works at Kennesaw Mountain, where he fell fatally wounded. Brigadier General Robert Latimer McCook ignored a severe wound to lead a charge that routed the Confederates at Mill Springs, Kentucky. Some months later, he was killed in an ambush by Confederate guerrillas while directing his command from an ambulance.

Ironically, the one career Army man in the family was an indifferent soldier. Major General Alexander McDowell McCook, a stout, amiable West Pointer, showed at Perryville and Stones River that he was neither quick nor resourceful enough for high command. But he shared the combativeness and personal courage characteristic of the McCooks and did not fall from official favor until Chickamauga in late 1863.

Patriarch Daniel McCook sits with rifle in hand surrounded by his nine sons. Killed in action along with their father were Daniel Jr., reclining at left center; Charles Morris, seated at Daniel's left; and Robert Latimer, standing behind his father. John James, second from right with hand to chin, died while in the Navy in 1842. Alexander McDowell sits facing his father.

bank of the river eastward through a series of hills to the Lebanon road, with Breckinridge's division in the forefront, backed up by Cleburne's division. To meet any attack from either Lebanon or Jefferson, the line faced due north, away from the Federal approach from Nashville.

Crittenden's corps approached Stones River in the late-afternoon gloom of December 29. The Federal cavalry, an inadequate force, had been unable to find out anything of value about the Confederate dispositions. In fact, Rosecrans told Crittenden that Bragg was retreating and ordered Crittenden to occupy Murfreesboro with one division and hold the rest of his corps on the west side of the river. Crittenden rode to the head of his column, where the divisions of Brigadier Generals Thomas J. Wood and John M. Palmer were forming lines of battle. They could all see, in plain view along the far bank of the river, a large part of the Confederate Army of Tennessee, and it was not retreating.

Crittenden, ignoring the odds against him, ordered Wood, with Palmer in support, to attack and occupy Murfreesboro. Wood protested that if he must take on Bragg's army with his lone division, it would best be done the next day during daylight. Crittenden agreed that an immediate movement would be risky, but he remained adamant — his order must be obeyed. Wood then sent Colonel Charles Garrison Harker's brigade splashing across the river into Confederate rifle fire. Harker's woefully outnumbered Federals managed to drive the Confederate skirmishers back about 500 yards, but then they ran headlong into Breckinridge's entire division and were stopped in their tracks. Wood could see that the attack was hopeless,

Braxton Bragg's aggressive cavalry commander, Joseph Wheeler, show here as a major general, was characterized by an Alabama neighbor as "the gamest little banty I ever seen. During the Confederate invasion of Kentucky, he had the reputation of riding farther and fighting harder th anybody else in either army. Three times wounded, he had 16 horses sh out from under him.

and Crittenden decided enough was enough. They described the situation in a message to headquarters and suggested that if General Rosecrans were there with them, he would not order an attack. Rosecrans concurred.

Bragg concluded correctly that the Federals would not attack then or the next day, December 30, and he ordered Wheeler's cavalry to harass the Federals' rear. Wheeler's men, who had been in the saddle almost continuously for three days, moved out shortly after midnight. They rode northward for about five miles, then turned west and at dawn struck Brigadier General John Starkweather's brigade at Jefferson, well behind the Federal lines. Although taken by

CAPT. JOHN W. MORTON'S
BATTERY

FORREST
CAVALRY CORPS.

Captain John W. Morton, whose name is prominently displayed on this Confederate battle flag, commanded a horse artillery company that had been armed with guns captured by Nathan Bedford Forrest in cavalry operations in western Tennessee. Renowned for their daring, the men of Morton's Tennessee Light Artillery fought with distinction during Forrest's assault on Federal lines of communication in December 1862.

could reach, was filled with burning wagons. The country was overspread with disarmed men, broken down horses and mules. The streets were covered with empty valises and trunks, knapsacks, broken guns and all the indescribable debris of a captured and rifled army wagon train."

From Lavergne, the raiders galloped six miles to the southwest. "We dropped like a tornado upon quiet little Nolensville," wrote Captain George K. Miller of the 8th Confederate Cavalry. "Here it was Lavergne repeated. We found squads of Yankees and some 150 wagons, mostly loaded with ammunition and medicines, together with several fine ambulances. These latter we preserved. The Yankees we sent on their way rejoicing, as paroled prisoners of war. We also had an immense deal of fun."

When Wheeler finally rode back into the Confederate lines, his men had destroyed all or parts of four wagon trains and had captured and paroled about 1,000 enemy soldiers. He brought back enough weapons to equip a brigade and many fresh horses for his command.

For the Federal soldiers in the lines near Murfreesboro, the night of December 29 had been a miserable one. The troops tried with little success to sleep, shivering in their wet clothes. They rose long before daylight but could not warm or dry themselves; orders had been issued that no fires were to be built. So the men prepared for a wearisome day of marching and countermarching. Since a battle was obviously imminent, they figured that the generals would — as usual — keep them busy closing gaps and changing positions; then the generals would redeploy everyone all over again. And the troops were

surprise, Starkweather's veterans resisted strongly. The Confederates had no time for a fight; they pressed on.

At noon, Wheeler's troopers rode up to Lavergne, seven miles northwest of Jefferson, and spied a rich prize — McCook's supply train of 300 wagons. In three columns, the Confederate horsemen stormed down on the wagons; the astonished Federals could offer only token resistance, and soon the train was Wheeler's.

Wheeler took 700 prisoners and destroyed nearly a million dollars' worth of Federal matériel. Lieutenant Colonel G. C. Kniffen of Crittenden's staff described the aftermath of the raid: "The turnpike, as far as the eye

kept tense and nervous by Confederate probing attacks along the line.

Early the next morning, Rosecrans and his staff appeared on the scene to oversee the disposition of forces. Crittenden's line was already anchored on the river to the north and extended across the Nashville Turnpike. Thomas was directed to place one of his divisions, that of Major General Lovell H. Rousseau, in reserve, while the other, commanded by Major General James S. Negley, advanced through the cedars to take position between Crittenden and the Wilkinson Pike to the south. Meanwhile, the Pioneer Brigade cut alleys and trails across the rugged terrain so that ammunition trains, ambulances and artillery could reach Negley's line.

McCook was ordered into place on the right of Negley to extend the line southward; as McCook's troops moved up to their assigned position, Confederate skirmishers dogged their advance. Rosecrans anxiously followed the troops' progress by the sound of musketry. Shortly after 7 p.m., the general was standing in the door of his headquarters, a log cabin near the Nashville Turnpike, when a Confederate sharpshooter hit one of his staff officers. Then Confederate shells began to descend. One of them exploded not far from Rosecrans; the next one to hit decapitated an orderly. Rosecrans decided to move. In a pouring rain, he led his generals up a slope to a spot among some trees, where the staff set up a crude shelter of fence rails and blankets. By then, McCook's troops had gained their position, extending the Federal line south to the Franklin road.

Rosecrans' orders to his corps commanders for the next day's fighting were delivered verbally and imprecisely; McCook would say

later that he learned the details when he read a newspaper account of the battle. Crittenden knew that he was to lead the attack against Bragg's right, but he did not know when to begin. Thomas had been told that he was to support Crittenden's attack. McCook, although he did not know the overall plan, was at least clear that his role was to maintain his position. His orders, as he later

Come out of that coat!!

Murfreesboro – Tenn.
Dec. 30. 1862

quoted them, were to "take a strong position; if the enemy attacks you, fall back slowly, refusing your right, contesting the ground inch by inch. If the enemy does not attack you, you will attack him, not vigorously, but warmly."

Rosecrans said later that he had intended more specific actions: Two of Crittenden's divisions, under Brigadier Generals Horatio Van Cleve and Thomas J. Wood, were to cross the river and punch through Breckinridge's forces on the Confederate right. At the same time, Thomas would launch the divisions of Negley and Brigadier General John Palmer against Polk in the Confederate center. While Negley and Palmer pinned down Polk's troops, Crittenden's divisions were to turn and drive southward in order to trap the Confederates in pincers — as Rosecrans wrote, "cutting off their retreat and probably destroying their army." As it happened, he would have the chance to execute his plan.

That evening, Rosecrans decided to see if he could deceive Bragg about the Federals' intentions. He ordered McCook to extend his right and build many campfires to make Bragg believe that the main threat was on that front, the Confederate left. The ploy was a trite one, used often by both sides. Still, it contributed to a fateful change in the Confederate dispositions.

Bragg was apparently fooled by the simple ruse. After spending the day in the field observing the various Federal moves, he called his corps commanders together at headquarters. He had concluded, he said, that the Federals were massing to strike the Confederate left; he then ordered a complicated series of adjustments not only to meet the threat there but to attack in force on the left. The Confederates spent much of the night groping through the darkness into their new positions.

Hardee took the divisions of McCown and Cleburne from behind Breckinridge, marched south behind Polk's line, crossed to the west side of the river and took position on Polk's left. Thus Hardee extended the Confederate line across the Franklin road, with McCown in front, supported by Cleburne. Wharton deployed his 2,000 cavalrymen on Hardee's left. When all this had been accomplished, the Confederate right was held only by Breckinridge's division, supported by Brigadier General John Pegram's cavalry brigade and a small reserve brigade called up from guard duty around Chattanooga.

As it happened, the two commanders had arrived at identical plans: to attack the other's right flank. And now the men on both sides settled down at last for a long night of waiting.

Before tattoo, one of the Federal regimental bands began playing; the strains of "Yankee Doodle," "Hail Columbia" and other popular Northern tunes drifted out to the Confederate lines. After a time, the Federal musicians yielded to a Confederate band, which played a series of Southern favorites. The musical exchanges continued until a Federal band struck up "Home Sweet Home." W. J. Worsham of the 19th Tennessee recalled that "immediately a Confederate band caught up the strain, then one after another until all the bands of both armies were playing 'Home Sweet Home.' And after our bands had ceased playing, we could hear the sweet refrain as it died away on the cool frosty air."

An Artist's Look at the Army of the Cumberland

Among the observers who traveled with the Army of the Cumberland was William Travis, a staff artist for *Harper's Weekly* and the New York *Illustrated News*. Gifted with a sharp and sometimes sardonic eye, Travis sketched the army in camp and on the march, in the flush of victory and the panic of defeat. Although General Rosecrans was his hero, Travis also had a rare feeling for the common infantryman, whose daily routine and hardships he carefully observed.

At the urging of a group of Cumberland veterans, Travis sat down after the War to record the army's history. From his sketches and his prodigious memory, he produced a 528-foot canvas panorama in 32 scenes mounted on rollers for easy handling and display. This monumental work — which included the scenes shown here — took touring through the Midwest, outstanding success. Veterans lauded work's realism, and nonveterans praise the words of one, its "rare beauty." popular acclaim pleased Travis — as Rosecrans' enthusiastic pronouncem that the artist was unrivaled in his "g conceptions of struggles on the battlefie

Artist William Travis depicted himself in the field, wearing makeshift campaign dress and riding a mule he called Big Fool. He sketched the army, he noted, "while the scenes were being enacted."

An officer embraces a loved one before leaving family and home to join the Army of the Cumberland. The columned portico, log cabin and distant mountains suggest that the setting is Kentucky

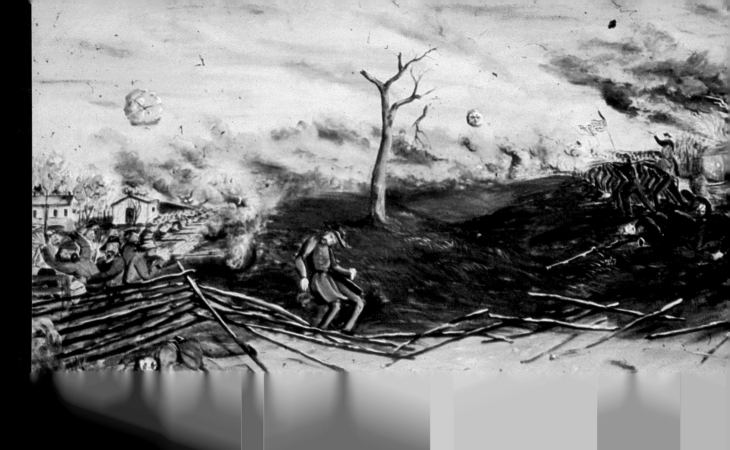

General Rosecrans, shown at center on a dappled gray, was an excellent rider known for the frequency of his mounted inspection tours. One observer said that Rosecrans was "in his saddle almost constantly, and ate as often on horseback as at table."

Nearing Nashville, units of Buell's army find that Confederates have set fire to a railroad bridge over the Cumberland. A pier of Nashville's ruined suspension bridge can be seen in the distance.

While a sentry paces his rounds and a black cook prepares a meal, Federal officers lounge in camp outside Nashville during the lull that preceded the army's march south to Murfreesboro.

Guards of a Union supply train try to beat back an attack by Confederate cavalrymen, visible under the trees. Lacking sufficient cavalry, Rosecrans relied on infantry to protect his supply wagons.

Fleeing the manor house of a Tennessee plantation under cover of darkness, runaway slaves
follow in the footsteps of a column of the Army
of the Cumberland, discernible in the distance.

On the first day at Stones River, part of the Union right flees before Confederates of McCown's and Cleburne's divisions. To the left, a mounted Union officer rallies an intact portion of the line.

Coming up to the front at Stones River as daylight
begins to fade, **General Rosecrans** (*far right*)
uses field glasses to scan Confederate artillery firing on a Federal battery in the middle distance.

Major General Alexander McDowell McCook,
on horseback at center, gestures with his sword
toward a distant line of advancing Confederates as
he tries to rally his shattered corps at Stones River.

An officer on horseback points out to a visitor one of the Union hospital camps hastily erected in Murfreesboro after the Battle of Stones River. Wounded soldiers can be seen hobbling between the tents.

The Fight for "Hell's Half Acre"

It was cold, damp and misty in the early-morning darkness of the last day of 1862. The two armies, drawn up for battle along icy Stones River, waited for word to begin the day's work. Some men slept. Others huddled uncomfortably in the mud of their bivouacs. The top commanders on both sides were prepared to attack.

The terrain and the position of the troops would prove crucial to the outcome of the battle. Bragg's line was split by the west fork of Stones River, an obstacle that would make lateral movement difficult. Despite the recent heavy rains, the river was fordable, though the waters between its steep banks could turn into an impassable torrent should the rains return. Fields of corn and cotton on both sides of the river alternated with dense glades of red cedars, their limbs touching the ground. The trees offered shelter for infantry but would make maneuver difficult.

The Federals' position appeared to be considerably stronger. On the Union left, Major General Thomas L. Crittenden had firmly anchored his left flank on Stones River. His lines ran through a four-acre clump of cedars known locally as the Round Forest. A deep and easily defended railroad cut ran through the woods about 100 yards west of the river. These features combined to make the Round Forest the strongest defensive position on the field. Before the day was over, the soldiers would be calling it "Hell's Half Acre."

On the Federal right, Major General Alex-ander McCook had been given a tough assignment. His left-flank division, commanded by Brigadier General Philip H. Sheridan, extended from the Wilkinson Pike south. To Sheridan's right was the division of Brigadier General Jefferson C. Davis, and on Davis' right — and the far right of the Federal army — was the division of Brigadier General Richard W. Johnson, whose line stretched to the Franklin Road, with one brigade straddling the road. McCook was supposed to hold his position while Crittenden attacked east of the river and Major General George Thomas carried out a limited attack from the Federal center. This would be no easy matter, for the Confederate line along the Franklin Road was perilously close to McCook's; in some places, the opposing pickets were only 100 yards apart, and bugle calls could be heard across the intervening space.

The commanders of both armies were counting on surprise. A powerful first blow was especially important to the Confederates, for Bragg did not have the resources to wage a long fight. Rosecrans, who had a slight edge in numbers, could call in Federal reinforcements from Nashville and from even farther north along the railroad to Louisville. The Confederates would have to win a victory on that day, December 31, or they were in danger of being driven from the field.

The two commanders would bring to the battle very different leadership styles. Rose-

road-brimmed hat worn into battle tones River by Private Clement sett bears the Lone Star insignia he 8th Texas Cavalry, better wn as Terry's Texas Rangers for regiment's founder, Colonel B. nk Terry. The Rangers, armed h shotguns, six-shooters and vie knives, captured intact a four- Union battery and, in hand-to- d combat, routed the cavalry pro- ing a Union supply train.

crans became excited in the heat of combat and tended to take personal charge wherever vital action was unfolding. Thus he risked losing control of the larger battle. Bragg, on the other hand, tended to let subordinates run the battle once he had done the planning. Though personally brave, he preferred to remain at his headquarters to receive reports and make decisions. But by staying to the rear, Bragg took the risk of losing touch with events. Moreover, he was inflexible: He had never developed the ability to modify plans once they had been set in motion.

The battle might have been decided at the outset if the Federal command had acted on a report of suspicious Confederate troop movements. General Sheridan, whose division anchored McCook's left, was sleeping behind a large fallen tree in the rear of his reserve brigade when he was roused at 2 a.m. by Brigadier General Joshua W. Sill, a close friend since West Point and one of Sheridan's brigade commanders. Sill reported that he had observed a large body of Confederate infantry, back-lighted by campfires, passing behind the Confederate line toward the Federal right. The units were apparently marching into attack positions. Though Sill did not know it, they were the two divisions of Lieutenant General William J. Hardee's corps, led by Major Generals J. P. McCown and Patrick R. Cleburne, whom Bragg at the

last minute had ordered to cross the river and extend the Confederate left flank.

Sheridan and Sill rode to McCook's headquarters and awakened their corps commander, who was curled up in a fence corner. McCook saw no cause for concern in Sill's observation; he said that Rosecrans was aware of the massing of the Confederates and that the plan would not be changed.

Sheridan returned to his division still worried. According to a sergeant in the 73rd Illinois, "Sheridan came along the line, on foot, and unattended. He called for the major, ordered him to rouse the men quietly, have them eat breakfast and form in line of battle at once. He personally visited each of his 12 regiments and saw that his orders were executed." Sheridan later wrote that he, too, had seen evidence of an impending attack: "All the recent signs of activity in the enemy's camp were hushed, a death-like stillness prevailing in the cedars to our front."

The alert was passed to the two other division commanders in McCook's corps, General Davis, in McCook's center, and General Johnson, on the far right. At this point, McCook acknowledged the threat and ordered Davis and Johnson to brace their troops to receive an attack at daybreak. Both generals relayed the orders to their brigade commanders, but even so, nobody was adequately prepared for what was to come.

Brigadier General August Willich, whose brigade was holding Johnson's extreme right flank, had anticipated the alert. During the night, he had been so apprehensive about Confederate activity on his front that he had ordered a patrol to reconnoiter the enemy lines. But when the scouts reported nothing of consequence, Willich had apparently relaxed and let down his guard. At about 5:30

a.m., Willich's brigade began its normal morning routine. The men, huddled in their overcoats, fell in for roll call, then boiled coffee and made breakfast, their arms stacked nearby. On their left, Brigadier General Edward N. Kirk's men were better prepared to meet an attack. They were up and carrying arms, with a strong picket line in their front. At first light, however, some of their artillery horses were unhitched and taken to water.

At about 6 a.m., as the darkness began to turn milky gray, an apparition appeared to the south and southwest of McCook's Federal positions. Blending in with the fog and mist, long gray lines of Confederates — the 11,000 men of the seven brigades of McCown's and Cleburne's divisions — formed like shadows in front of the protective cedars. Noiselessly, they began to move toward the Federal lines, McCown's men on

the left and Cleburne's on the right, following 500 yards behind. "We could see the enemy advancing over the open country for about half a mile in front of our lines," General Kirk later reported. "They moved in heavy masses, apparently six lines deep. Their left extended far beyond our right, so as to completely flank us." Slowly at first, then faster, and finally at the double-quick, the Confederates attacked across the cotton fields and cornfields. They held their silence until they came within close range of Johnson's Federals. Only then did the Confederates scream their wild Rebel yell.

The seven Confederate brigades descended on the two Federal brigades with overwhelming force. A private in the 36th Illinois recalled, "It seemed that the whole Confederate army burst out of a piece of woods immediately on the front." To make matters worse for Willich's brigade, Willich had just

General William Rosecrans (secon at right of altar) and some of his s attend a Mass conducted by Rosecrans' personal chaplain, Father P rick Trecy, in their Stones River headquarters. Rosecrans, who ha converted to Catholicism while at West Point, heard Mass every mor ing and carried a crucifix and rosa with him into battle.

gone to the rear to look for General Johnson, leaving his troops leaderless.

Kirk sent word of the assault to Johnson and then ordered the 34th Illinois to counterattack the oncoming Confederates. "This solitary regiment never wavered," he wrote, "but steadily advanced until they closed with the enemy and it became a hand-to-hand fight. The balance of my line now became engaged and fought most bravely against fearful odds. No other proof is needed of the fierceness of the conflict at this point and the stubborn tenacity with which our men fought, than the fact that considerably more than one half of some of these regiments were shot down before yielding an inch of ground." Kirk called for help from Willich's brigade, but the leaderless troops were confused and unable to respond.

The fighting was brief but ferocious. Five color-bearers of the 34th Illinois were killed in quick succession before the Confederates seized the colors and pushed the Federal regiment back. Kirk's troops fired several volleys point-blank into the massed gray infantry, but the Confederates kept driving ahead, their casualties littering the ground behind them. The Confederates reached Kirk's line first. It held for only a few minutes, then broke. The men panicked. Kirk himself sustained a wound that six months later would take his life. As he was being carried to the rear, he shouted to his men to get out or be captured by the Confederates.

To Kirk's right, the Confederates had reached Willich's line and smashed into it just as Willich's men were reaching for their stacked arms. To the left, the demoralized men of Kirk's brigade had begun running for the rear, trampling comrades underfoot. The Confederate onslaught and the pell-mell retreat of Kirk's men proved too much for Willich's regiments. They also broke and fled. "A complete panic prevailed," wrote Colonel William H. Gibson, who was commanding Willich's brigade in his absence. "Teams, ambulances, horsemen, footmen and attachés of the army, black and white, mounted on horses and mules, were rushing to the rear in the wildest confusion."

Brigadier General James E. Rains's brigade swept around the Federal right flank. In the assault, Rains was shot from his horse, mortally wounded, but his men pushed on. To make matters worse for the beleaguered Federals, the Confederate cavalrymen of Brigadier General John Wharton rounded the Union flank at a gallop and wreaked havoc in the enemy's rear. Routed Federals became intermingled with the advancing Confederates — a situation that spelled disaster for General Willich. When Willich rode back through the chaos to find his brigade, he found himself shouting orders to a group of soldiers he thought were his. He was mistaken. Almost at once, the Confederates shot his horse and took him prisoner.

Though the contest was uneven in these first minutes of battle, men on both sides fought with great courage. While pursuing Willich's troops, Sergeant A. Sims, a color-bearer of the 10th Texas Dismounted Cavalry, was startled when a fleeing Federal color-bearer turned and confronted him. Sims rushed forward, planted his banner at the feet of his enemy and lunged for the man's standard with his free hand. At that instant, both color-bearers were shot, and a soldier wrote that they "fell in the agonies of death waving their banners above their heads until their last expiring moments." The Texans kept their standard, but not before one man

Confederates dash headlong into point-blank Federal fire in a painting by the Tennessee artist Gilbert Gaul that exemplifies the desperate fury of Confederate bayonet charges at Stones River. "The Rebels came on screaming like demons," reported Union General Philip Sheridan; a Confederate officer wrote that his regiment "leapt forward like men bent on conquering — or dying in the attempt."

Major General John P. McCown, a West Pointer from Tennessee, was disparaged by General Bragg as "lacking the capacity and nerve" for a responsible command. Yet Bragg chose to launch the Confederates' dawn attack at Stones River with McCown's 4,500-man division.

Major General Patrick R. Cleburne, whose division helped turn the Federal right flank at Stones River, was an Irish immigrant who had served in the British Army. A savage fighter and a respected commander, Cleburne became known as "the Stonewall Jackson of the West."

who rushed to save it was also shot down.

Within half an hour, the two Federal brigades ceased to exist as effective fighting units. Kirk had lost 483 men killed and wounded, and another 376 captured. Willich's brigade suffered 463 casualties, and 700 of its troops surrendered. The brigades had lost nearly all of their artillery. Most of the survivors did not stop retreating until they reached the Nashville Pike and the railroad cut, three miles to the rear. Private Joseph T. McBride, a Confederate soldier captured in the skirmishing before the battle, witnessed the rout. Shocked, he called out to the fugitives, "What you running for? Why don't you stand and fight like men?" A fellow prisoner turned and shouted at him, "For God's sake, Joe, don't try to rally the Yankees! Keep 'em on the run!"

The Federal flank had been turned. The flight of Johnson's troops had exposed the right flank of General Davis' division. Davis, hearing the commotion on his right, ordered Colonel P. Sidney Post's brigade to bend back part of its line 90 degrees to face the enemy sweep. Meanwhile, Johnson's reserve brigade, commanded by Colonel Philemon P. Baldwin, moved up from its bivouac a mile behind the original front. About a quarter of a mile to the right of Post, Baldwin's men formed a line of battle among the cedars and limestone outcroppings, loaded their muskets and waited for the Confederates.

Before long, Davis' newly adjusted line — now forming an arc that faced from southeast to southwest — was hit hard by the four brigades of General Cleburne's division. In the first line were the brigades of Brigadier Generals St. John Liddell and Bushrod Johnson. These troops were closely followed by Cleburne's other brigades under Brigadier Generals Lucius E. Polk and S.A.M. Wood.

Davis' troops, though greatly outnumbered, refused to yield, and their stalwart defense robbed the Confederate drive of its momentum. The Confederates could not push through, and their attack began to falter. One of the Federal regiments, the 29th Indiana, even launched a counterattack, "determined," wrote their major, "to stop the sweeping tide or die."

In the Confederate center, meanwhile,

part of General Leonidas Polk's corps had joined the assault. But Polk's advance was proving haphazard. The night before, Polk had reorganized his command in a way that proved to be more confusing than effective. As a result, elements of Major Generals Benjamin F. Cheatham's and Jones M. Withers' divisions were committed piecemeal. And the failure of command coordination caused the first Confederate setback of the day.

Around 7 a.m., Polk had thrown the Alabama brigade of Colonel J. Q. Loomis against the Federal line where it was manned by the brigades of Colonel William E. Woodruff on Davis' left flank and Joshua Sill on Sheridan's right. Loomis drove the Federal line backward but exposed his right flank to enfilading artillery and musket fire from Sill's position. As a result, reported Colonel Woodruff, the Confederates "were mowed down as grass beneath the sickle."

The brigade of Colonel Arthur H. Manigault was supposed to move up in support on Loomis' right, but Manigault failed to advance. Loomis' men were forced to retreat across an open field dotted with their own dead and wounded. As the Alabamans fell back through Colonel A. J. Vaughan's brigade of Texans and Tennesseans, they were jeered. One of Loomis' men angrily retorted, "You'll soon find it the hottest place you ever struck!"

The misadventures of Loomis and Manigault were largely the fault of their divisional commander, General Cheatham, who was subsequently alleged by some of his fellow officers to have been drunk that morning. Cheatham allowed Loomis to advance an hour late and then let Manigault waste another hour before joining the assault.

General Bragg did what he could to correct his lieutenants' mistakes, but it was too late. For the moment, the opportunity to overwhelm the Union right wing had been lost.

Far to the north, on the Federal left flank, General Rosecrans was initiating his own attack. He had risen early, awakened his staff officers and heard Mass with his chief of staff and fellow Catholic, Lieutenant Colonel Julius P. Garesché. Crittenden had joined them on a knoll, and together they had watched the men of Brigadier General Horatio Van Cleve's division splash across Stones River and advance toward Major General John C. Breckinridge's division, the only remaining Confederate force east of the river.

Rosecrans had appeared unconcerned about the sounds of firing from the south. Ignoring the distant thud of artillery, he had ridden over to Brigadier General Thomas Wood, who was preparing to follow Van Cleve across the river, and gave the order to move out. Wood, a veteran of Shiloh and Perryville, sat astride his horse with a bandaged foot — the result of a recent wound — and with crutches slung from his saddle.

As Wood left to carry out Rosecrans' directive, he remarked sardonically to Crittenden, "Goodbye, general, we'll meet at the hatter's, as one coon said to another when the dogs were after them."

Rosecrans had then returned to his headquarters, where he learned from Garesché that Wharton's cavalry had rounded the Federal right flank. Rosecrans was still unconcerned; he assumed that McCook could handle the situation.

Around 7 a.m., the sound from the Federal right had become deeper and louder. Some compared it to the rumble of heavy wagons; others thought it was more like a big wind

By 8 a.m. on December 31, Hardee's Confederate troops have driven in the Federal right wing, crushing Willich's and Kirk's brigades. Polk has started a piecemeal advance in the Confederate center, while on the right, Breckinridge stands idle awaiting Crittenden's Federals, who are crossing the river to attack

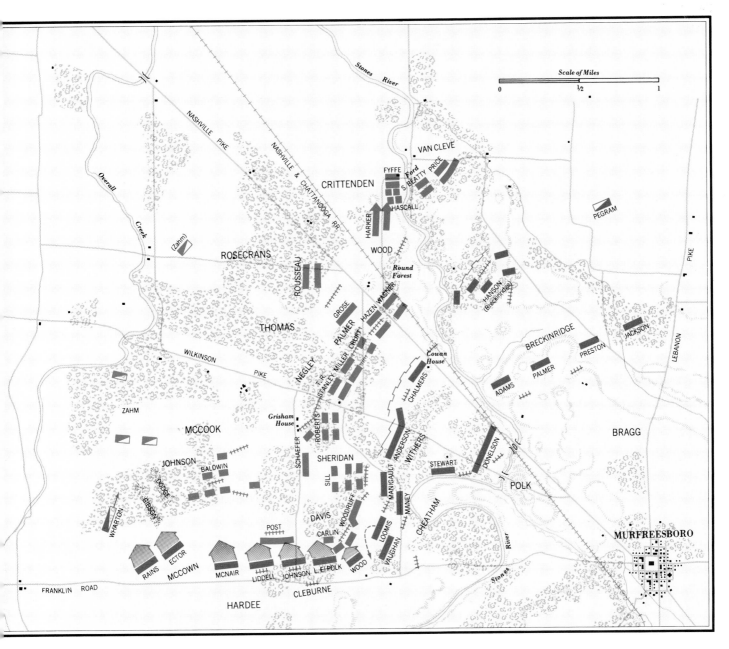

preceding an intense storm. Fugitives from McCook's units began filtering back past the ranks of the Federals drawn up in reserve in the center, north of the Wilkinson Turnpike. The woods behind Major General James Negley's division, on Sheridan's left, began to fill with teamsters, stragglers, mules and the impedimenta of the rear echelon of Johnson's routed division.

From his position behind Negley's division, Henry V. Freeman, an officer in the Pioneer Brigade, described what he saw: "The debris was drifting back rapidly, cannon and caissons, and remnants of batteries, the horses of which had been killed, were being hurriedly dragged off by hand. There were men retiring with guns, and men without their guns; men limping, others holding up blood stained arms and hands; men carrying off wounded comrades; and faces blackened with powder, and in some cases stained with blood. Riderless horses dashed out of the woods which still partly hid the combat. Over all arose, near at hand or more faintly from the distance, the yells of the Rebel victors."

By now, Rosecrans was at last becoming anxious about his right flank. He sent Cap-

tain Elmer Otis, commander of his cavalry escort, to find out what was happening to McCook. Otis sent back word that the Federal right wing had been broken. But his courier was followed by one from McCook himself. This officer said only that McCook was heavily pressed and needed assistance, an appraisal so understated that it misled Rosecrans into believing that things were moving according to plan. "Tell General McCook," he ordered the courier, "to dispose his troops to best advantage and hold his ground." Turning to his staff, Rosecrans said, "It is working right. If he holds them, we will swing into Murfreesboro and cut them off."

The truth began to come clear when Rosecrans learned of Willich's flight and capture. Next came an appeal from McCook for reinforcements. "So soon," Rosecrans remarked gravely. "Tell General McCook I will help him."

Now deeply concerned, Rosecrans direct-ed George Thomas to send Major General Lovell H. Rousseau's division to Sheridan's right rear. Rosecrans also ordered Van Cleve to stop his advance, to recross the river and to assemble near the railroad, leaving a brigade to guard the fords. Wood's supporting division had not yet begun its crossing, and Colonel Charles G. Harker's brigade and that of Brigadier General Milo S. Hascall quickly moved toward a position on the Federal far right to reinforce McCook.

The Confederates, meanwhile, continued to batter the new Federal flank, formed by the brigades of Colonels William P. Carlin and William E. Woodruff of Davis' division and Sill's brigade of Sheridan's division.

Sheridan later described this part of the action: "The enemy attacked me, advancing across an old cotton field in Sill's front in heavy masses, which were furiously opened upon by Captain Asahel Bush's battery from Sill's line and by the batteries of Captains

Henry Hescock and Charles Houghtaling, which had an oblique fire from a commanding position in rear of my center. The effect of this fire on the advancing column was terrible, but it continued on till it reached Sill's right, when my infantry opened at a range of 50 yards. For a short time the Confederates withstood the fire, but then wavered, broke, and fell back toward their original line."

Confederate losses were so severe that corps commander Polk had to commit additional troops, the Texans and Tennesseans under Colonel Vaughan and Brigadier General George Maney. Colonel William H. Young, who led the charge of his 9th Texas, reported: "I ordered the regiment to move forward with a shout, both of which they did, *à la* Texas (colors in hand)." The first charge broke against Sill's line. Sill's brigade then counterattacked the shattered Confederates, driving them back across the open ground. "In this charge," Sheridan wrote

sadly, "the gallant Sill was killed, a rifle ball passing through his upper lip and penetrating the brain." However, added Sheridan, who was to lose all three of his brigade commanders by midday, "the enemy's discomfiture was such as to give us an hour's time."

The Confederate charge might have been successful but for a mistaken command. Private Sam Watkins, who attacked with the 1st Tennessee Infantry of Maney's brigade, said that his comrades "raised a whoop and yell, and swooped down on those Yankees like a whirl-a-gust of woodpeckers in a hail storm." But while approaching Sheridan's lines, the Tennesseans were ordered to cease fire and heard nearby Confederates shouting at them, "You're firing on your own men." At the same time, other Confederates were yelling, "Shoot, they're Yankees!" Confused, the Confederates were driven back.

Watkins was wounded in the arm during the assault. As he walked back to a field hospital, he overtook a wounded comrade who had lost his left arm. "His face was as white as a sheet," Watkins wrote. "The frazzled end of his shirt sleeve appeared to be sucked into the wound. I said 'Great God' for I could see his heart throb and the respiration of his lungs. He was walking along, when all of a sudden he dropped down and died without a struggle or groan."

Soon after the repulse of Vaughan and Maney, their division commander, Cheatham, re-formed his four brigades and made another assault upon Sheridan and what was left of Davis' division. Cleburne's division had by now outflanked Davis on his right, and at the moment of Cheatham's renewed attack, Cleburne drove in on the Federals from their flank and rear.

Davis' brigades had fought fiercely, but

now they gave way and headed for the rear — another disaster for the Federals. The flight of Davis' troops exposed Sheridan's right flank, and Sheridan had to act quickly to save his division.

To protect his flank, he swung his line to the right like a gate until it rested perpendicular to his original position. To Sheridan's right lay Rousseau's division, which was moving up alongside him; and strung out to Sheridan's left were Negley's division and that of Major General John Palmer. By 10 a.m., the Federal line had been hammered into a V shape, with the left side facing east and the right facing roughly west.

Sheridan's troops manned the apex of the salient — and the Confederates gave them no rest. Sheridan's left was defended by the Illinois regiments of Colonel George W. Roberts' brigade. Roberts' officers were cut down one by one. Captain Alexander F. Stevenson was fighting in the 42nd Illinois in support of an exposed artillery unit, the 1st Illinois Light Battery, under Captain Charles Houghtaling. Stevenson recalled the toll: "Death and blood everywhere," Stevenson reported. "Colonel Harrington, bravely leading the 27th Illinois, was struck by a piece of shell, which tore the jaws from his face; Lieutenant Colonel Swanwick, of the 22nd Illinois, wounded and unable to be moved; nearly 40 per cent of the 42nd and 22nd killed or wounded; gallant Captain Houghtaling carried away barely alive, the blood, as it flowed from his wound, leaving a track on the stone; and Lieutenant Taliaferro, who had never flinched in the hottest fire, but who seemed to grow in stature as the fire became more intense, shot dead between his cannon. Houghtaling's men refused to leave their

guns and defended them with their revolvers, sabers and ramrods, till they were finally overpowered and many taken prisoner." Among the dead was Colonel Roberts, the brigade commander.

Under such pressure, Sheridan was forced to conduct a fighting withdrawal northward. He was able to re-form his line just north of

the Wilkinson Pike, keeping his right flank in contact with Rousseau. But the Confederate attacks remained relentless.

By midmorning, Bragg's army had suffered casualties that it could ill afford. One third of Hardee's corps had been killed or wounded, including six brigade and regimental commanders. Polk's corps had suffered 30 per cent losses, most of them in Maney's and Vaughan's assaults on Sheridan's lines.

Nevertheless, Bragg had reason to be pleased. The enemy's right flank had been destroyed, and although Sheridan and Rousseau clung tenaciously to their new positions, their units had been badly mauled. The Confederates were continuing to attack with spirit, and one more great effort might roll up the Federal lines.

At 10 a.m., Bragg received a request for reinforcements from Hardee. The only Confederate reserves west of Stones River were some cavalry units. Bragg had to look to his right flank for help — to the unengaged troops of Breckinridge's division. Bragg immediately told Breckinridge to send two brigades to support Hardee. Breckinridge refused, explaining that he was about to be attacked by a large Federal force. Breckinridge was under the mistaken impression that Van Cleve, whom Rosecrans had recalled at least two hours earlier, was still advancing toward the Confederate right wing.

Lacking evidence to contradict Breckinridge, Bragg ordered him to attack and drive the Federals back across Stones River. Breckinridge slowly advanced and made the startling discovery that there were no longer any enemy troops east of the river. About this time, however, Bragg received a report from Brigadier General John Pegram's caval-

ry, patrolling far to the Confederate right, that a large column of Federal infantry was approaching from the north, down the road from Lebanon. Accepting the scouts' information without attempting to confirm it, Bragg canceled his order to Breckinridge to send the two brigades to reinforce Hardee. This decision may have saved Rosecrans, for as it turned out, the report was erroneous: No Union column was on its way.

While Bragg was sorting out his problems with Breckinridge, Rosecrans was dashing from place to place, shoring up his lines in the face of heavy fire. On the left, he rode to Colonel Samuel W. Price, whose brigade was in position to resist any attack by Breckinridge from across the river. "Will you hold this ford?" Rosecrans demanded.

"I will try, sir!"

"Will you hold this ford?" Rosecrans repeated, his voice loud and agitated.

"I will die right here," Price responded.

"Will you *hold* this ford?"

"Yes, sir!"

Rosecrans wheeled his gray horse, and with his blue-overcoat tails flying, galloped off to see for himself how the men were faring on the right flank. By now, elements of Crittenden's corps were moving along the battlefront, extending the Federal right wing beyond the new lines begun by Rousseau and Sheridan. Cleburne and Cheatham continued to press the Federals, looking for a weak spot to exploit.

The Federal brigade of Colonel John Beatty had been ordered by Rousseau to take a position in a clump of cedars to the right of Sheridan's beleaguered brigades. Beatty was ordered to hold the position, he wrote, "until hell freezes over." The colonel deployed his four regiments as ordered. On his right was a brigade of tough and determined United States Regulars under Lieutenant Colonel Oliver Shepherd. Beatty recalled later: "I take position. An open wood is in my front; but where the line is formed, the cedar thicket is so dense as to render it impossible to see the length of a regiment. The fight begins, with the roar of the guns sounding like continuous pounding on a thousand anvils. The 3rd Ohio, the 88th and 42nd Indiana hold the position and deliver their fire so effectively that the enemy is finally forced back."

Beatty then was hit again by McCown's division, which had been re-formed and re-supplied. Beatty's regiments fought for an hour more, until Beatty learned that Sheridan to his left and Shepherd to his right had been forced to withdraw. "I conclude," he wrote, "that the contingency has arisen to which General Rousseau referred — that is to say, that hell has frozen over."

While Beatty was heavily engaged, Rosecrans around 11 a.m. rode up to Rousseau's position. There he met Sheridan, who was leading his men rearward. The bandy-legged little Sheridan was furious; he was retreating again not because he had been defeated but because his men were nearly out of ammunition. Earlier, Wharton's Confederate troopers, rampaging in the Federal rear, had almost captured McCook's ammunition train; it had had to be withdrawn to save it.

Sheridan began swearing vividly, but Rosecrans cut him short. "Watch your language," Rosecrans warned Sheridan. "Remember, the first bullet may send you to eternity." Sheridan later remembered that Rosecrans appeared pale and drawn, but that "he seemed fully to comprehend what had befallen us. His firmly set lips and the calmness with which his instructions were delivered inspired confidence in all around him.'

Sheridan was forced to withdraw north to the Nashville Pike, and his retreat left a yawning gap in the Federal line, offering the Confederates an opportunity that they immediately tried to exploit. Hardee sent his troops plunging into the opening, but they were unable to take advantage of the breakthrough. On either side of the break, under intense fire, Rousseau's and Negley's Federals executed an artful withdrawal, pulling back and uniting on high ground along the Nashville Pike. Negley's withdrawal, however, left Palmer's division dangerously exposed in front of the densely wooded Round Forest. Palmer's brigades formed a salient, but the position seemed weak — vulnerable to the cross fire of Confederate batteries. Seeing his chance, General Polk acted quickly, committing his last two brigades in an effort to smash the salient. He ordered Brigadier Generals James Chalmers and Daniel S. Donelson to make the assault.

The men of Chalmers' Mississippi brigade rose from a shallow trench they had dug two days earlier and advanced across an open field, supported by Breckinridge's artillery from the other side of the river. The charging Confederates were swept by rifle fire from the Round Forest and from cannon that Rosecrans had concentrated just behind that Federal strong point. Chalmers was hit by a shell fragment and had to be carried from the field. Under a devastating fire, his now-disorganized brigade faltered and fell back.

Donelson's Tennesseans took up the attack. Working their way around the garden fences of the burned-out Cowan farmhouse, they pushed back the exposed Federal units south of the Round Forest. But now Donelson's men found their line split in two. To

The Strong-hearted Regulars

Sprinkled through the Federal armies were units of the regular U.S. Army. They were elite outfits, admired for their professionalism, their esprit — and even their uniforms, which many volunteer regiments copied.

The lone brigade of Regulars at Stones River was led by Lieutenant Colonel Oliver Shepherd, a West Pointer with 20 years' service. When the battle began, the Regulars — as was often the case — were held in reserve, as a trump card to be played in an emergency.

As the Federal right wing started to crumble, the Regulars were committed. For hours they resisted Confederate thrusts while retreating Union soldiers streamed through their lines. At noon came an order to advance. General George Thomas pointed to a thicket of cedars and said: "Shepherd, take your men in there and stop the Rebels."

Changing front as smartly as if on parade, the Regulars marched into the cedars, where their determined stand bought time for the Federals to re-form. Finally, exposed to fire on three sides, they withdrew. "Men were falling all along the line," wrote an adjutant, "but not one turned his back to the enemy."

The cost had been dear. Of the brigade's 1,600 men, two out of five were wounded or dead — double the casualty rate that day for the rest of the Army of the Cumberland.

U.S. REGIMENTAL COLORS
CARRIED AT STONES RIVER

MODEL 1858 U.S. ARMY HAT

U.S. ARMY CORPORAL'S FULL-
DRESS FROCK COAT

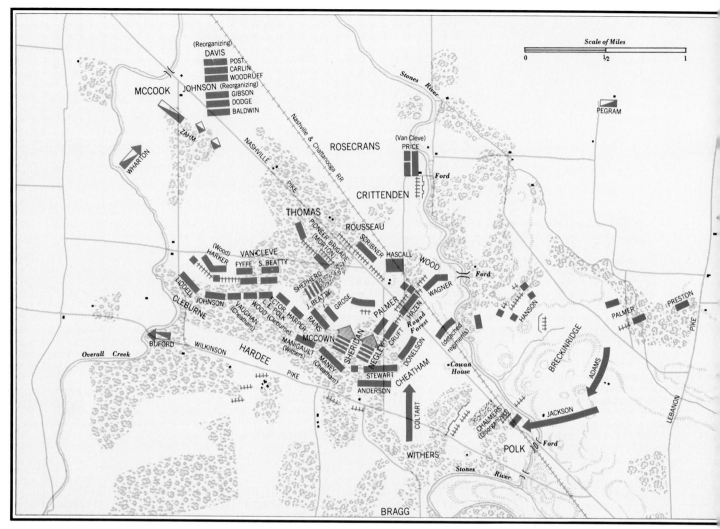

the right of the Cowan house, the 16th Tennessee and part of the 51st Tennessee were repelled with heavy losses. In one company, all of the officers and noncommissioned officers were killed or wounded, and the shattered survivors were brought out under the command of Private Wright Hackett. Donelson's men to the left of the Cowan house — the 8th, 38th and the remainder of the 51st Tennessee — struggled forward. Sergeant J. M. Rice, the color-bearer of the 8th Tennessee, was shot but crawled forward, desperately holding up his flag. A second bullet killed him, and another soldier took up the colors. The men never reached the Round Forest but were forced to take cover in a cedar brake near the Wilkinson Pike, a position they held for the rest of the day despite a steady pounding from Federal batteries.

The two Confederate brigades paid a heavy price in casualties for the gallant ferocity of their attacks. The 8th Tennessee of Donelson's brigade lost 306 of its 472 men; the 16th Tennessee lost 207 men of the 402 who started the advance.

By noon, the ever-changing hook-shaped Federal line had the Round Forest at its apex and its right flank pushed back almost to the Nashville Pike. Rosecrans, using the time between Confederate charges, had somehow managed to rebuild his right. Elements of Wood's and Van Cleve's divisions, which had been diverted from the canceled attack on Breckinridge, were now in position on the right flank of Rousseau's division and were repelling renewed attacks from Hardee's tiring corps. The stand of these Federal units allowed the shattered divisions of Davis and Johnson to reorganize along the Nashville

roximately noon, the Confed-
advance on their left has al-
un its course and the Federals,
riginal line folded back on the
ille Pike like the blade of a jack-
are stubbornly defending a sa-
hat is centered on the Round
t. On the Federal left, Critten-
brigades have been recalled
ast of the river to reinforce the
al right flank, and Confederate
s on the Round Forest, by
ers' and Donelson's brigades,
een repulsed.

Pike and the nearby railroad. Sheridan had replenished his ammunition from Critten-den's train and was moving to bolster the Federal right flank.

Bragg had learned that the Federals were strengthening their right, and he reasoned that now their left flank should be weak-er. With Hardee's exhausted troops stalled on the Federal right, Bragg determined to smash the enemy left, which now ran north-east from the Round Forest to Stones Riv-er. He seems not to have considered that the Federals, within their hook-shaped line, would be able to shift troops easily to defend any point of attack. And Bragg gave up any notion of reinforcing Hardee.

Thus far, repeated Confederate attacks against the Round Forest had gotten no-where. This failure was largely the result of a rocklike defensive stand by a valiant Federal brigade in Palmer's division, commanded by Colonel William B. Hazen. Hazen's troops, deployed astride the Nashville Pike and the railroad, had held the forest since early morning. Hazen's brigade had had plenty of help. Improvising skillfully, Rosecrans had ordered regiments to Hazen's salient with-out regard for their original organization or commanders. At various times in the long fight, Hazen would be supported by units from Sheridan, Negley, Wood, Palmer, Van Cleve and Rousseau. Except for a slight shift to the left during Polk's assaults just before noon, Hazen's four regiments — the 41st Ohio, 110th Illinois, 9th Indiana and 6th Kentucky — maintained their position un-der almost constant attack while the Federal lines changed around them. Now they were in the forefront of the Federal defense.

At 1 p.m., Bragg sent an unequivocal or-der to Breckinridge to send him four bri-gades at once. Until the fresh units could arrive, a lull descended upon the battlefield. Once more using the time to advantage, Rosecrans and Thomas strengthened the Federal left by gathering all available artil-lery on a rise behind Hazen in the Round Forest, while Hazen braced his men for yet another onslaught.

Colonel William Hazen was a tough West Pointer, class of 1855. He had served on the frontier until severely wounded by Coman-ches in 1859. His wounds kept him on sick leave for about two years, but in 1861 he returned to active duty as commander of the 41st Ohio, which he led at Shiloh and Perry-ville. He was a strict disciplinarian and an unemotional, even cold leader; his troops disliked him but admired his ability.

During a morning attack, Hazen's horse had been shot out from under him, but he had calmly gotten up and directed his men on foot until he could find another mount. At one point, Hazen was told that the 41st Ohio and 110th Illinois were running low on am-munition. He ordered the Buckeyes to "fix bayonets and hold your ground." The Illi-nois troops reported that they had no bayo-nets. Hazen told them to use their muskets as clubs but to give not an inch. They held.

For an hour or more in midafternoon, Confederate attacks on the Round Forest ceased, although Hazen reported that "a murderous shower of shot and shell" contin-ued to rain on his position from several direc-tions. By 4 p.m., the firing on the Federals' right had stopped entirely. Looking out in that direction, the Federal troops in the Round Forest saw long blue lines drawn up between dark patches of cedar; their com-rades were standing to, alert to the Confeder-ates who lay facing them at a distance. The

General Rosecrans rides into the thick of the fray to direct fire against a Confederate charge at Stones River. The Union left is shown firmly anchored on the river and the railroad running to Nashville, while fresh troops in the foreground move up to secure Rosecrans' right.

gray lines of weary soldiers were almost indistinguishable from the clumps of Confederate dead and dying. East of the Round Forest, the Federals watched fresh Confederate troops crossing the river, which was still rising from the recent rains. Daylight had begun to fade, but there was time enough for one last desperate Confederate charge.

The new Confederate units were the four brigades that Bragg had demanded of Breckinridge and was sending to Polk for another attack on the Federal salient. The first detachment contained the brigades of Brigadier Generals Daniel W. Adams and John K. Jackson. Polk had no illusions about the strength of the Federal position. He also realized, as he later wrote, that "the opportune moment for putting in these detachments had passed." But he went ahead anyway, ordering a new assault on the Round Forest. In doing so, Polk made a serious error. Instead of waiting for all four brigades to come up, he sent in the first two with no support. Jackson and Adams aligned their brigades in perfect order and attacked across a field littered with mangled grayclad bodies from the earlier charges of Chalmers and Donelson.

Hazen, from his position in the forest, watched with alarm. "At about 4 p.m. the enemy again advanced upon my front in two lines," he later reported. "The battle had hushed, and the dreadful splendor of this advance can only be conceived, as all description must fall vastly short. The enemy's right was even with my left, and his left was lost in the distance. He advanced steadily and, as it seemed, certainly to victory."

Hazen called on Rosecrans for more help, and he received it. Reinforced, he ordered his infantrymen to hold their fire. The Confederates advanced under a heavy pounding from the Federals' massed artillery. When they came into close range, a single scathing volley of rifle fire was enough to disperse the grayclad lines. Polk's attack had been magnificent to see, but the results were dismal. Polk later reported that in less than an hour after it had crossed the river, the 8th Mississippi of Jackson's brigade lost 133 of its 282 men; that Adams' brigade had suffered equally from the combined Federal artillery and rifle fire; that the consolidated regiment of the 13th and 20th Louisiana had lost 187 of 620 men. Adams himself was wounded in the arm by a shell fragment.

As the men of Jackson's and Adams' brigades fell back, they saw Breckinridge arriving on the field at the head of the two remaining brigades. One was commanded by Brigadier General William Preston; the other was led by Colonel Joseph B. Palmer, acting in place of the regular commander, Brigadier General Gideon J. Pillow, who was on detached duty. These brigades, too, would be sacrificed, for the Confederate command was by now obsessed with the Round Forest and determined to have it, no matter what the cost. Polk ordered Breckinridge to attack immediately.

Once more the Confederates formed into battle line. Once more they charged across the fallow cotton field, cracking and breaking the brittle stalks, leaping over the hundreds of dead and wounded comrades who had come this way before. By now the Federals had emplaced 50 cannon on the rise behind the forest, and all of them were firing as fast as their crews could reload. Once more the Confederates fell back before the scythelike Federal volleys, leaving behind another layer of bodies on the field. Spencer Tally of the 28th Tennessee recalled, "In the fading light, the sheets of fire from the enemy's cannon looked hideous and dazzling."

The action looked much better from the Federal lines. On the crest of the hill behind the forest, Rosecrans and his commanders watched with elation as the Federal artillery chewed holes in the Confederate formations. Glancing about, General McCook suddenly realized that too many senior officers were gathered in an exposed position. He called out, "This is a nice mark for shells. Can't you thin out, men?" Rosecrans ignored the suggestion. "It's about as safe on one side as another," said George Thomas, but he moved, and McCook and his staff followed.

At one point, Rosecrans sensed that Hazen's men were beginning to falter. With Colonel Garesché and others riding close behind him, Rosecrans galloped recklessly down the slope, ignoring the heavy Confederate counterfire. An aide who was following saw a cannonball flash past Rosecrans and strike Garesché full in the face. The headless body, spouting blood, remained in the saddle for 20 paces before sliding to the ground. Confederate fire cut down several others in Rosecrans' party.

Rosecrans, unaware that staff members had perished behind him, rode on into the midst of the Federal regiments in the Round Forest. There he was urged by some infantrymen to be more careful. The commander responded bluntly: "Men, do you know how to be safe? Shoot low! But to be safest of all, give them a blizzard, and then charge with cold steel!"

When someone told Rosecrans of Garesché's death, he showed no visible emotion. "Brave men die in battle," he said. "Let us push on. This battle must be won!"

This unusual framed memento of the War, shown here almost twice its actual size, is composed of 16 tiny photographic portraits, known as gemtypes, of soldiers who served in the 36th Illinois Volunteers. Ten of these men were wounded at Stones River on the morning of December 31.

An actual sketch, made on the spot by one of the Special Artists of Frank Leslie's Illustrated Newspaper.

Mr. Leslie holds the copyright and reserves the exclusive right of publication.

In fact, Rosecrans was deeply affected by his friend's death. After the battle, he cut the buttons from his own uniform and saved them in an envelope marked "Buttons I wore the day Garesché was killed."

The repulse of Breckinridge's brigades ended the fighting for the day. The merciful order to cease fire was given near sunset by General Hardee, who, unable to do any more with his own troops, rode up to see what was happening on Polk's front. When he saw the proportions of the futile slaughter, he ordered Breckinridge to call it quits.

In spite of their terrible losses, the Confederates were generally convinced that victory was theirs. Hardee's report on the day's work did not betray any sense of defeat. "For three miles in our rear, amid the thick cedars and the open fields, where the Federal lines had been originally formed, their dead and their dying, their hospitals, and the wreck of that portion of their army marked our vic-

torious advance. Our bivouac fires were lighted at night within 500 yards of the railroad embankment, behind which their disordered battalions sought shelter."

Actually, Rosecrans' battalions were far from disordered; they simply collapsed in place, exhausted by the day's fight. Rosecrans returned to his cramped log-cabin headquarters along the Nashville Turnpike and called a conference of his corps commanders. The blustery winter night was cold, and the cabin offered welcome shelter.

Rosecrans was by no means convinced that the day had been successful. He began the meeting by discussing the possibility of retreat and then solicited the opinions of his senior officers. According to his own account, Rosecrans received advice to retreat from McCook and from the cavalry commander, General Stanley. Thomas and Crittenden were noncommittal but vowed to support Rosecrans in whatever decision he made. According to another account, George Thomas fell asleep during the meeting. But when the word "retreat" was mentioned, he awoke with a start, opened his eyes, looked about with a fierce gaze that had often struck terror into skulkers and muttered, "This army does not retreat." Rosecrans left the meeting and personally scouted a route of withdrawal as far northwest as Overall Creek, one mile behind his lines. Then, on his return, he announced that there would be no retreat.

Rosecrans had decided to stay where he was for at least the next day. He lacked rations and other supplies, but he did have enough ammunition for one more day's fighting, and he knew his army was willing to defend itself at least that long. He sent off a wagon train protected by an escort of 1,000 men to Nashville to evacuate some of the wounded and to return with the essentials for the army's existence.

Bragg, still in his headquarters, wanted to believe he had won a major triumph. And he found all the confirmation he needed in reports of the Federal wagons moving north toward Nashville. Convinced that he would catch the Army of the Cumberland strung out along the road to Nashville on New Year's Day, Bragg sent a telegram to Richmond: "The enemy has yielded his strong position and is falling back. God has granted us a happy New Year."

Then, without changing the disposition of his troops in any way, Bragg went to bed.

The Craft of Field Artillery

Invented by former Federal officer Robert Parrott, the Parrott Rifle was accurate and — because its barrel was made of cast iron rather than costly bronze — inexpensive to manufacture. A Parrott was able to hit a target at 2,500 yards, about twice the range of a smoothbore gun.

During the Civil War, artillery at[tained] a lethal effectiveness that did m[uch to] make the conflict one of the dead[liest in] history. In support of infantry at[tacks,] the guns hurled solid shot and [explo]sive shell into the enemy's form[ations] and fieldworks. On the defense, [artil]lery could be even more destru[ctive,] firing shotgun-like canister bla[sts at] close range into oncoming infa[ntry.] And rival gunners tried to anni[hilate] each other with counterbattery fir[e, us]ing shot and shell to wreck gun[s and] blow up caissons full of ammun[ition.]

In a camp near Murfreesboro, Bridge's Battery of the Illinois Light Artillery, serving in General Rosecrans' army, turns out in full regalia with all its g[uns]

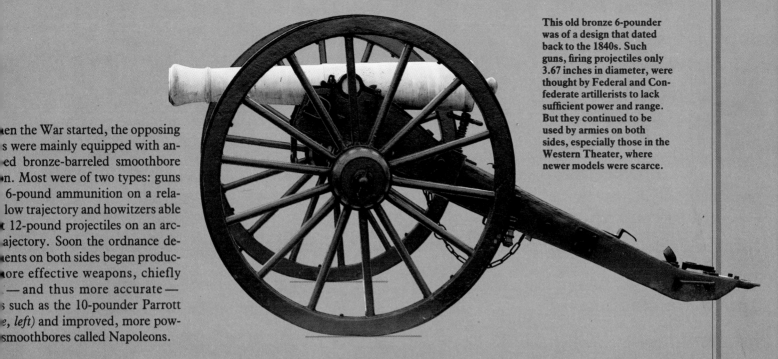

This old bronze 6-pounder was of a design that dated back to the 1840s. Such guns, firing projectiles only 3.67 inches in diameter, were thought by Federal and Confederate artillerists to lack sufficient power and range. But they continued to be used by armies on both sides, especially those in the Western Theater, where newer models were scarce.

en the War started, the opposing s were mainly equipped with an- ed bronze-barreled smoothbore n. Most were of two types: guns 6-pound ammunition on a rela- low trajectory and howitzers able 12-pound projectiles on an arc- ajectory. Soon the ordnance de- ents on both sides began produc- ore effective weapons, chiefly — and thus more accurate — s such as the 10-pounder Parrott *e, left)* and improved, more pow- smoothbores called Napoleons.

s. The battery was equipped with a variety of weapons: two 12-pound Napoleons *(left)*, two 3-inch ordnance rifles *(middle)* and a pair of 6-pounder guns.

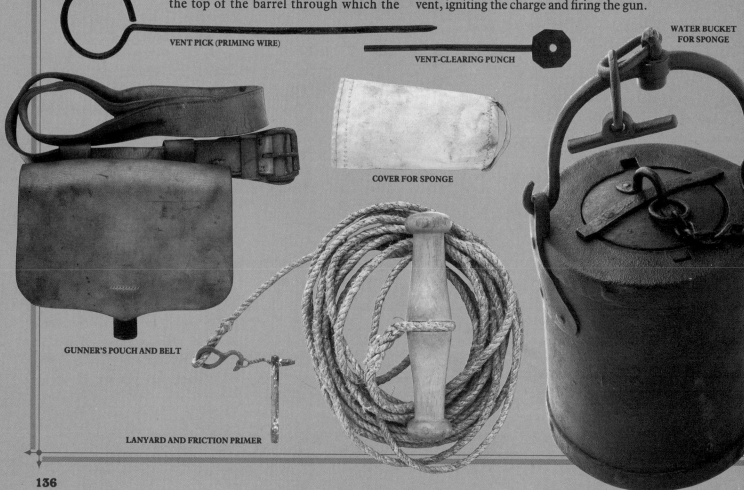

SPONGE-AND-RAMMER

WORM-AND-BRUSH FOR CLEARING BARREL

TRAIL HANDSPIKE

The Tools of a Well-drilled Team

Experienced gunners working together with precision (*opposite*) could load and fire a fieldpiece twice a minute — even when enemy fire was bursting about them.

The tools of the gunners' perilous trade were simple. The largest was a sponge-and-rammer. The sponge swabbed the barrel, removed leftover powder and doused any residual sparks that might prematurely ignite the next charge. The rammer forced the round down the barrel.

A punch was used to clean out the vent in the top of the barrel through which the powder charge was fired; a leather finger stall closed the vent during loading to extinguish any sparks still there, and a pick was rammed down the vent to rip open the powder bag after loading. The trail handspike served as a lever to aim the heavy barrel. To fire the piece, a gunner put the friction primer, a two-inch brass tube containing combustibles, including phosphorus, into the vent. He then pulled the lanyard, which yanked a wire through the phosphorus. The matchlike flash traveled down the vent, igniting the charge and firing the gun.

VENT PICK (PRIMING WIRE)

VENT-CLEARING PUNCH

WATER BUCKET FOR SPONGE

COVER FOR SPONGE

GUNNER'S POUCH AND BELT

LANYARD AND FRICTION PRIMER

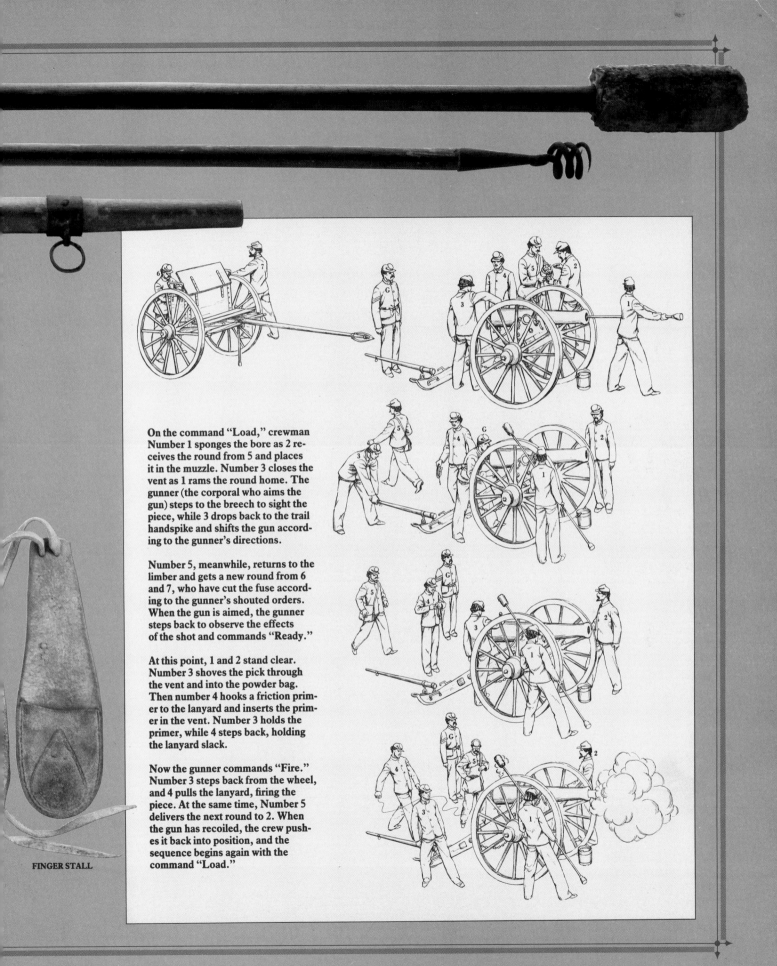

On the command "Load," crewman Number 1 sponges the bore as 2 receives the round from 5 and places it in the muzzle. Number 3 closes the vent as 1 rams the round home. The gunner (the corporal who aims the gun) steps to the breech to sight the piece, while 3 drops back to the trail handspike and shifts the gun according to the gunner's directions.

Number 5, meanwhile, returns to the limber and gets a new round from 6 and 7, who have cut the fuse according to the gunner's shouted orders. When the gun is aimed, the gunner steps back to observe the effects of the shot and commands "Ready."

At this point, 1 and 2 stand clear. Number 3 shoves the pick through the vent and into the powder bag. Then number 4 hooks a friction primer to the lanyard and inserts the primer in the vent. Number 3 holds the primer, while 4 steps back, holding the lanyard slack.

Now the gunner commands "Fire." Number 3 steps back from the wheel, and 4 pulls the lanyard, firing the piece. At the same time, Number 5 delivers the next round to 2. When the gun has recoiled, the crew pushes it back into position, and the sequence begins again with the command "Load."

FINGER STALL

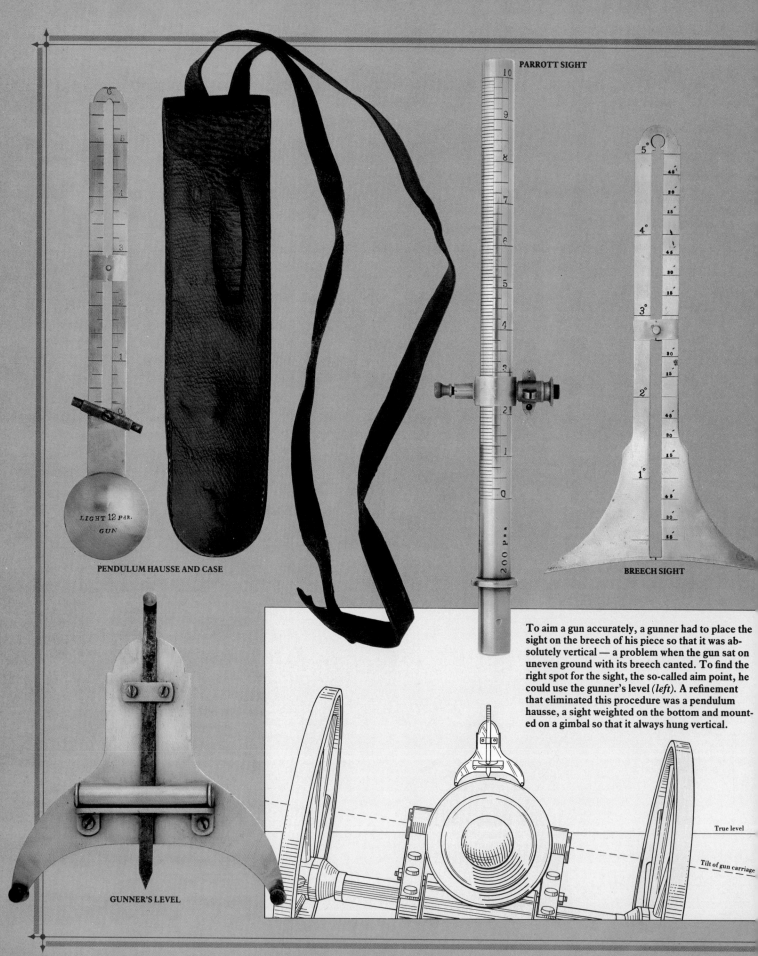

PARROTT SIGHT

PENDULUM HAUSSE AND CASE

BREECH SIGHT

GUNNER'S LEVEL

To aim a gun accurately, a gunner had to place the sight on the breech of his piece so that it was absolutely vertical — a problem when the gun sat on uneven ground with its breech canted. To find the right spot for the sight, the so-called aim point, he could use the gunner's level (*left*). A refinement that eliminated this procedure was a pendulum hausse, a sight weighted on the bottom and mounted on a gimbal so that it always hung vertical.

True level

Tilt of gun carriage

TABLE OF FIRE ARMS
10-PDR. PARROTT GUN
Charge, 1 lb. of Mortar Powder

ELEVATION In Degrees	PROJECTILE		RANGE In Yards	TIME OF FLIGHT In Seconds
1	Case Shot,	10½ lbs.	600	
2	Case Shot,	10½ lbs.	930	3
2¾	Shell,	9¾ lbs.	1100	3¼
3⅞	Shell,	9¾ lbs.	1460	4¾
4½	Shell,	9¾ lbs.	1680	5¾
5	Shell,	9¾ lbs.	2000	6½
6	Shell,	9¾ lbs.	2250	7¼
7	Shell,	9¾ lbs.	2600	8¼
10	Shell,	9¾ lbs.	3200	10¾
12	Shell,	9¾ lbs.	3600	12⅞
15	Shell,	9¾ lbs.	4200	16⅞
20	Shell,	9¾ lbs.	5000	21⅞

CARE OF AMMUNITION CHEST

1st. Keep everything out that does not belong in them, except a bunch of cord or wire for breakage; beware of loose tacks, nails, bolts, or scraps.
2nd. Keep friction primers in their papers, tied up. The pouch containing those for instant service must be closed, and so placed as to be secure. Take every precaution that primers do not get loose; a single one may cause an explosion. Use plenty of tow in packing.

(This sheet is to be glued to the inside of Limber Chest Cover.)

The Precise Art of Aiming

To hit his target, a gunner needed to determine three things: the distance to the target, how much to elevate the gun's barrel to throw the projectile that far and how much a cross wind might push the shot off line.

Many Civil War artillerymen became uncannily good at estimating distance and the effects of wind. But aiming the piece for long-range shooting called for some special aids. First, from a table of fire (*above*), a gunner found the correct elevation in degrees for the distance to his particular target. Next, he placed on the breech of the gun one of the commonly used sights (*opposite, top*); each was essentially a length of brass notched with an elevation scale in degrees, and each carried a sliding peep hole. Making sure that the sight was perfectly vertical (*opposite, bottom*), the gunner slid the peep hole along the rod to the predetermined degree mark. Then he peered through the hole down the barrel and lined up his target. Finally, he elevated the barrel of the gun until the tip of the muzzle was in the line of sight. Now the gun was ready to fire.

Table-of-fire charts, which were pasted on the inside of the ammunition chests carried by limbers and caissons, provided gunners and shell handlers with vital information concerning the performance of various types of guns and ammunition, including the elevations needed for various ranges and the number of seconds the projectile would be in flight.

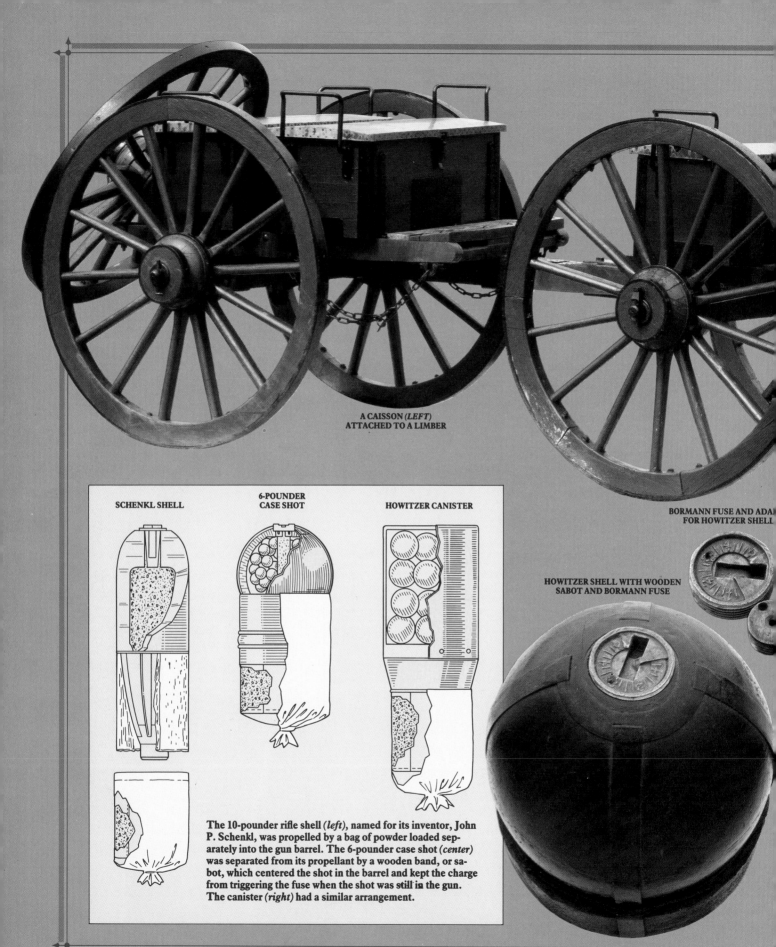

A CAISSON (*LEFT*) ATTACHED TO A LIMBER

SCHENKL SHELL

6-POUNDER CASE SHOT

HOWITZER CANISTER

BORMANN FUSE AND ADA[
FOR HOWITZER SHELL

HOWITZER SHELL WITH WOODEN
SABOT AND BORMANN FUSE

The 10-pounder rifle shell (*left*), named for its inventor, John P. Schenkl, was propelled by a bag of powder loaded separately into the gun barrel. The 6-pounder case shot (*center*) was separated from its propellant by a wooden band, or sabot, which centered the shot in the barrel and kept the charge from triggering the fuse when the shot was still in the gun. The canister (*right*) had a similar arrangement.

An Array of Lethal Ammunition

The simplest artillery projectile used in the Civil War was solid shot — deadly iron balls employed mostly at long range. For short-range work there was canister — tin containers that disintegrated when they were fired, scattering a hail of bullets.

Charged projectiles — shells and case shot — exploded after reaching the target. Shells burst into lethal fragments; case shot held a payload of metal balls. These projectiles, used at medium and long ranges, carried either impact fuses or time fuses. The best time fuse, named for a Belgian ordnance expert, was the Bormann, which contained a slow-burning powder. The gunner punched a hole in its thin metal top at one of the marks indicating the burning time. The flame from the gun's discharge went into the hole, starting the fuse. Less reliable but cheaper were paper fuses, which could be cut to size to burn for a specified number of seconds.

PAPER TIME FUSES

Frankford Arsenal.
1864.
5 SECOND FUZES.
To take a fuze from the package, tear the paper at top by raising the piece of tape, and press against the small end of the fuze with the finger.

PACKETS OF
PAPER TIME FUSES

GUNNER'S CALIPERS USED TO
MEASURE AMMUNITION SIZE

BRASS FUSE PLUG DESIGNED TO
HOLD PAPER FUSES IN SHELLS

BORMANN FUSE WRENCH FOR SEATING FUSES
IN SHELLS AND CASE SHOT

PUNCH EMPLOYED TO SET
BORMANN FUSES

HAVERSACK USED TO CARRY
ROUNDS FROM THE LIMBER

Across Stones River and Back

"I can never forget, whilst I remember anything, that you gave us a hard-earned victory, which, if there had been a defeat instead, the nation could scarcely have lived over."

ABRAHAM LINCOLN TO MAJOR GENERAL WILLIAM S. ROSECRANS

As the short winter twilight faded to darkness, the cannonading ceased, and the din of musketry subsided to an occasional popping. Rain fell, and cold crept across the battlefield, into the cedar brakes, among the boulders, into the torn bodies of the wounded and dying. The cold completed the bonding of the dead to the earth, freezing bodies to the ground with their blood.

Many soldiers were too stunned to comprehend and too cold to move. Others wandered the field looking for friends, helping the wounded or removing the dead. There were acts of kindness among foes on the frozen field. With a few companions, Private J. T. Tunnell of the 14th Texas Dismounted Cavalry built a fire in a sinkhole, where they were protected from the wind and enemy observation. "Among the wounded," Tunnell recalled, "was a Yank quite young, shot through the breast. We divided rations with him, and next morning our young Yank, with assistance to rise, could sit up awhile."

Colonel William Hazen, commander of the gallant Federal brigade in the Round Forest, left the shattered wood toward dusk and searched along the railroad tracks for the body of his friend, Colonel Garesché. When he found the headless corpse, he saw that rigor mortis had caused one of Garesché's arms to reach out. Hazen took the cold hand in his own, removed Garesché's West Point class ring, retrieved Garesché's well-thumbed copy of *The Imitation of Christ* and ordered a detail to move the body to a more

appropriate place. Later in the evening, Hazen looked on, shivering, draped in a bloody blanket proffered by a Confederate deserter, as soldiers dug Garesché's grave.

Few of the dead received immediate burial, for there were thousands of wounded scattered across the field demanding attention. They called out for help, for a fire, for water, for their mothers, for God's mercy — or begged to be shot to escape their agony. Soldiers did what they could, regardless of the color of their uniforms. Henry Freeman, a Federal officer, spent the night near two severely wounded Confederates, frequently giving them water from his canteen. When he returned to them in the morning, the officer wrote later, "both were dead. Some kindly hand had covered their faces with their hats and spread blankets over the remains."

When the fighting ended, chaos reigned in Murfreesboro. Ambulances pushed their way through crowds of soldiers, prisoners and the walking wounded. The streets were tangled with supply wagons and the carriages of those who had come to retrieve their husbands, sons, brothers and friends. Captain Spurlock of the 16th Tennessee, who had visited his parents on the night of the 30th, was returned to them dead by men of his regiment. One woman came to claim the bodies of four of her sons.

Many of the Federal wounded embarked on a jolting 30-mile wagon trip to Nashville that would consign them to prolonged ag-

142

A **boyish-looking private in a Zouave company of the 19th Illinois Infantry rests his hand on a volume of United States history in this cracked ambrotype. The young soldier's regiment waded across Stones River under fire to lead a climactic Federal counterattack in the final hour of fighting at Murfreesboro.**

ate attacks that he was sure would come in the morning. He consolidated his battered formations west of the river, pulling his troops back from the Round Forest and strengthening his right flank. He ordered his left-flank division, now led by Brigadier General Samuel Beatty in place of Van Cleve, who had been wounded, to recross the river and occupy a ridge that commanded two fords on the east bank.

Rosecrans worked through the night, personally supervising the placement of units and reassuring his men. He seemed to be everywhere. Several men of the 21st Ohio, who had fought grimly all day in the Federal center, were gathered around a roaring fire when Rosecrans, still wearing his blood-stained uniform, suddenly loomed out of the darkness. "You are my men," he said, "and I don't like to have any of you hurt. When the enemy sees a fire like this, they know 25 or 30 men are gathered about it. I advise you to put it out." Seconds later, a shell descended and burst just beyond the fire.

Rosecrans knew that his commanders also needed encouragement. Rations were scarce, and there was enough ammunition for only one more day's fighting. "Our supplies may run short, but we will have our trains out tomorrow," Rosecrans told his generals. "We will keep right on, and eat corn for a week, but we will win this battle. We can and will do it."

The night passed slowly. Men on both sides, kept awake by the rain and the cold, waited miserably for the dawn, when the armies would again collide.

When General Bragg awoke on New Year's Day, he was shocked to learn that the Federals were still in their lines. He had been so

ony. When the maimed soldiers finally arrived, they faced the routine horrors of army hospitals. John Fitch, Provost Marshal of Nashville, recalled that at the infamous Brickhouse Hospital, three tables were in constant use for amputations; severed limbs and flesh were tossed through the windows into waiting carts. The floors were slick with gore.

Rosecrans went to work to bolster his shaken army against the renewed Confeder-

certain Rosecrans would retreat that he had no plan for continuing the battle. And instead of going to work to devise a strategy, he sank into a deep lethargy of the kind that had seized him before, at Shiloh and Perryville.

Bragg spent the day doing menial tasks and issuing inconsequential orders. He had his infantrymen salvage abandoned Federal equipment, and he sent cavalry units to reconnoiter the Federal rear. They reported heavy traffic in Federal soldiers and wagon trains headed for Nashville, and for a time Bragg was encouraged to believe the Federals were retreating after all. But it turned out that the wagons, strongly escorted to protect them from Confederate raiders, were simply removing the wounded.

Polk's corps moved unopposed into the abandoned Round Forest, which now harbored pitiful masses of dead and wounded soldiers and animals. Bragg ordered Breckinridge to recross Stones River and take up his original position on the right. Just before daybreak, Breckinridge sent a brigade under Colonel Joseph B. Palmer back across the river to join other troops that had remained on the Confederate far right. Throughout New Year's Day, Palmer's men kept up a series of skirmishes with the Federals. But Bragg did not order the general attack that his soldiers expected — and dreaded.

The Federals were also much relieved by the unforeseen respite. "We were all in line expecting every moment a recommencement of the fearful struggle," General John Beatty wrote in his diary. "Both armies want rest; both have suffered terribly. Here and there little parties are engaged burying the dead, which lie thick around us. Now the mangled remains of a poor boy of the 3rd Ohio is being deposited in a shallow grave.

Generals Rosecrans and Thomas are riding over the field, now halting to speak words of encouragement to the troops, then going on to inspect portions of the line. A little before sundown, all hell seems to break loose again, but it is simply the evening salutation of the combatants."

Most of the Federals got no supper that night. Yet despite their hunger, their spirits were rising. General Beatty observed: "We all glory in the obstinancy with which Rosecrans has clung to his position."

For a time, it looked as though January 2 would be an uneventful repeat of New Year's Day. Bragg, again hoping that Rosecrans had withdrawn during the night, sent skir-

ease with their pipes, cigars and a
dle, men of the Washington Light
tillery's 5th Company — the on-
company of the famed Confederate
ttalion to fight in the west — pre-
nt a picture of relaxed confidence
a March 1862 photograph. In the
st Confederate charge at Stones
ver, 5th Company troops galloped
the contested ridge and held it
th their 12-pounder Napoleons un-
their ammunition gave out.

mishers forward at dawn. But they retired immediately on finding the Federals still manning their positions.

As an early rain turned to sleet, Bragg ordered his artillery to probe the Federal center on the west side of the Round Forest. The 22 Confederate guns spread across the Nashville Pike blazed away for a while; a Federal officer wrote that cannonballs rolled up the Nashville Pike "like balls on a bowling alley." The Federal batteries responded with vigor, leaving Bragg in no doubt about his enemy's determination to stand fast.

Suddenly, it occurred to Bragg that if he could place some guns on the high ground east of the river, in front of Breckinridge, he

could enfilade the Federal position on the west side of the river. He dispatched staff officers to reconnoiter the area. At noon, the officers returned and reported that the ridge Bragg wanted for his guns was already occupied by Colonel Samuel Beatty's Federal division and its artillery.

This spawned a new worry in Bragg's mind: If Beatty's guns were in position as reported, they now threatened Polk's troops, athwart the Nashville Pike, with enfilading fire from across the river. Suddenly — and belatedly — combative, Bragg decided that Breckinridge must take the high ground from Beatty; Bragg summoned his general to headquarters.

On his own initiative, Breckinridge had spent the morning testing Beatty's lines to find out what the Confederates were facing. He had portions of the 18th Tennessee Infantry prod Beatty's left and right flanks. Breckinridge himself rode with a party along the river, then proceeded forward far ahead of the Confederate main lines. Coming under sniper fire, the general ordered his soldiers to drive in the Federal pickets so he could calculate the location and strength of Beatty's forces.

Breckinridge saw that Beatty's brigade was strongly emplaced in two lines on the ridge, facing east. The Federals enjoyed the advantages not only of high ground but also of abundant cover and a wide-open field of fire. In addition to Beatty's artillery, six guns of the 3rd Wisconsin Artillery were placed on a hill just west of the river and commanded the open ground in front of the ridge that Beatty occupied.

Thus, when he responded to Bragg's summons to headquarters, Breckinridge was staggered by his general's order to attack

93RD OHIO VOLUNTEER INFANTRY (BALDWIN)

Dandridge, Kinesaw Mt.

Chattahoochie River.

93ᵈ REGᵗ O.V.I.

Antioch Church.

Stone River. Liberty Gap. Chickamauga

Browns Ferry

Mission Ridge, Resaca, Laurel Hill.

Franklin, ATLANTA

18TH OHIO VOLUNTEER INFANTRY (ST

Stone River.

18ᵗʰ REGT.
O.V.I.
U.S.A.

Carrying the Colors
on the Battlefield

The flags unfurled at Stones River by the Federal Army of the Cumberland (*above and near right*) and the Confederate Army of Tennessee (*opposite*) consisted of the six primary designs shown here. While the Union flags were adapted from standard patterns, the diverse Confederate flags were the work of independent corps commanders whose units had been merged into one army.

Each flag was defended by a color guard of up to eight noncommissioned officers — the best men in the regiment. A flag's value was practical as well as emotional: It served as a guide for infantrymen moving into a battle line and as a rallying point for a disorganized unit. However, flags also were often the only targets visible to enemy marksmen through the gray smoke of battle, a fact confirmed by the terrible mortality rate of the brave men who carried them.

1ST TENNESSEE VOLUNTEERS (POLK)

5TH COMPANY, WASHINGTON ARTILLERY (BRAGG)

17TH TENNESSEE VOLUNTEERS (HARDEE)

RKANSAS VOLUNTEERS (MCCOWN)

the formidable position. Bragg wanted the assault launched at 4 p.m. so that darkness would interfere with any Federal counterattack. Bragg promised the support of Polk's artillery across the river to the southwest and of the cavalry brigades of Wharton and Pegram on Breckinridge's right flank. But Bragg did not offer any other reinforcements.

Breckinridge protested vehemently. He sketched the enemy positions in the mud to show Bragg how the Federal artillery was deployed to devastate the planned attack. Bragg's only response was to observe that Breckinridge's Kentuckians had thus far suffered less than the others and that it was now their turn to show their mettle. When Breckinridge continued to object, Bragg got angry; he always turned belligerent when his judgment was questioned. He dismissed Breckinridge, telling him, "Sir, my information is different. I have given an order to attack the enemy in your front and expect it to be obeyed."

Bragg's harsh discipline and uncertain leadership had been fostering resentment among his men ever since he had taken command of the army. And now, in this poisonous atmosphere, Bragg's order very nearly touched off a mutiny.

Bragg seems to have been particularly critical of Breckinridge's Kentucky soldiers, perhaps because of the failure of Kentucky civilians to enlist in the army during Bragg's invasion of that state. At any rate, Breckinridge's Kentuckians believed themselves to be especially afflicted by Bragg's truculent ways, none more so than Brigadier General Roger W. Hanson's 1st Kentucky Brigade.

The Orphan Brigade, as the unit came to be called because its native state was in enemy hands, was a veteran outfit that had fought well at Shiloh and Hartsville. But the men of the Orphan Brigade had somehow earned a reputation for self-pity and overconfidence; it was said they were extremely touchy and saw a slight in everything short of a tribute. Such tendencies did not mix well with Bragg's penchant for blaming his men for any failure.

Colonel Basil Duke of the 2nd Kentucky Cavalry wrote that the Kentucky men took Bragg's habitual criticism personally and responded in kind: "His hatred and bitter, active antagonism to all prominent Kentucky officers have made an abhorrence of him part of a Kentuckian's creed."

The increasingly tense relationship had almost come to a head a week before the Stones River battle. At issue was the case of Private Asa Lewis of Hanson's 6th Kentucky, who had been absent without leave. Lewis was returned to Murfreesboro by a bounty hunter and brought before a court-martial on December 20.

His story was not unusual. His 12-month enlistment had expired, and he felt that an edict requiring his regiment to serve either for three years or for the duration of the War did not apply to him since he had not reenlisted. Moreover, he was urgently needed at home. His father had died, leaving his mother with three young children. Lewis was the family's only means of support. He had applied for a furlough to go home and plant a crop, but his request was denied. Unfortunately for Lewis, he had deserted once before and had been let off with a reprimand. For a second desertion, the sentence was death.

Bragg approved the sentence and ordered General Hanson to carry out the execution on December 26. The outraged Kentucky officers campaigned to have the sentence commuted. Breckinridge himself visited Bragg to plead for Lewis' life, charging heatedly that the execution would be murder. But Bragg was determined to make an example of the deserter.

At 11 a.m. on December 26, Lewis was paraded in front of the Orphan Brigade in a wagon. His coffin followed in a second wagon. With his brigade drawn up in an open-ended square around him, Lewis faced the

While leading the charge of his Kentucky troops, Brigadier General Roger W. Hanson became the fourth general officer to suffer mortal wounds at Stones River. Hanson died two days after the battle despite the ministrations of Mary Breckinridge, his division commander's wife, who was helping to nurse the Confederate wounded in Murfreesboro.

firing squad, his hands bound behind him. Breckinridge dismounted and walked over to the condemned private. They exchanged a few whispered words. Then the general remounted and rode to one side. The firing squad performed its duty. As Lewis fell dead, Breckinridge pitched forward on his horse, deathly sick; members of his staff caught him and saved him from a fall.

Now, just one week later, Bragg was sending Breckinridge and the Kentuckians to certain destruction. Hanson was so enraged at what he considered to be a deliberately murderous order that he proposed to go to headquarters and kill Bragg.

But Breckinridge, a patriot and an obedient soldier, quieted his officers and set to work deploying his 4,500 men, most of whom had just arrived from their positions across the river. In the first line, on the left, he placed Hanson's Orphans. On the right were Palmer's Tennesseans, now led by their original commander, Brigadier General Gideon J. Pillow, who had returned from detached duty. In support, 200 yards to the rear was a brigade led by Colonel Randall Gibson and another under Brigadier General William Preston.

While the infantry was moving into position, Breckinridge and Captain Felix Robertson, Bragg's artillery chief, argued about the deployment of Robertson's guns. Breckinridge wanted Robertson's artillery to move up with the attacking troops along with Breckinridge's own guns, but Robertson said that Bragg had ordered him to stay to the rear until the high ground was taken. In the end, Robertson kept his guns in the rear, while Breckinridge placed his division artillery between the two lines of infantry.

Another problem arose: Breckinridge was

unable to coordinate his attack with the cavalry on his right flank. Two staff officers sent by Breckinridge to locate Wharton and Pegram were unsuccessful. Wharton first learned of the attack when he saw the infantry advancing into position. Pegram may have learned of the attack, but he was not in position when it began.

At 3 p.m., Braxton Bragg rode up to Polk's headquarters, informed Polk of the imminent attack on the east bank and ordered him to prepare his artillery to support Breckinridge. Polk opposed the attack and told Bragg that he did not consider his line threatened by the Federals on the ridge. But his argument got nowhere, and he broke off the discussion to deploy his guns as ordered.

The Confederate preparations were clearly visible to the men of Beatty's division on the ridge. Beatty had deployed, from left to right, the brigades of Colonel William Grose, Colonel James P. Fyffe and Colonel Samuel Price, whose right flank was anchored on the river. Colonel Benjamin Grider commanded the reserve brigade.

General Rosecrans also was aware of the Confederate concentration; he and Crittenden began calling reinforcements to the area about 3 p.m. The divisions of Brigadier Generals Jefferson C. Davis and Milo S. Hascall, Hazen's brigade and that of Charles Cruft in Negley's division were moved up to Beatty's left flank on the east bank of the river. Meanwhile, Crittenden's chief of artillery, Major John Mendenhall, began massing more guns on the hill across the river from Beatty's troops; eventually, he would have 58 pieces there.

Polk's artillerymen opened fire at 4 p.m. During the cannonading, the commanders on both sides moved to good observation

Kentucky's Exiled Soldiers

The most remarkable unit to serve with General Braxton Bragg's Confederate Army of the Mississippi was the 1st Kentucky Brigade, an infantry unit famed for its fighting qualities, its devotion to the Confederacy and to Bourbon whiskey — and its long years of homeless exile.

The men of the brigade were exiles because Kentucky, although deeply divided in its sympathies, was occupied by Union forces shortly after the War began. These Kentucky volunteers in the Confederate cause were unable to return home, like most other Confederate soldiers, when on leave or recuperating from wounds. Viewing the brigade's bedraggled survivors after one hard battle, the unit's best-loved commander, former U.S. Vice President John C. Breckinridge, called them "my poor orphans." Such they remained throughout the War, and in later years the veterans took pride in saying they had served in the "Orphan Brigade."

Exile for the Kentucky soldiers began as soon as they volunteered. Forced to flee their native soil, they trained under their first commander, General Simon Bolivar Buckner, across the border in Tennessee. In time, the brigade gained such a reputation for hard fighting that the various Confederate generals in the Western Theater vied for its services, shuttling the unit between the Vicksburg area on the Mississippi River and Bragg's Te[n]ee campaigns. As a consequence, the [Ken]tuckians were in the thick of a remark[able] number of bloody battles, as the flags [deco]rating the song sheet at right attest.

Eventually, more than three fourt[hs of] the Orphans became casualties, includ[ing a] number of their best officers, whose n[ames] appear in the plaques on the song s[heet.] During the fierce campaign for Atlan[ta in] 1864, nearly 1,000 Orphans were k[illed,] wounded or captured, and the bri[gade] ceased to be an effective fighting force[.]

**MAJOR GENERAL
JOHN C. BRECKINRIDGE**

A BATTERED BUGLE OF THE 2ND REGIMENT

SONG SHEET OF THE KENTUCKY BRIGADE'S ANTHEM

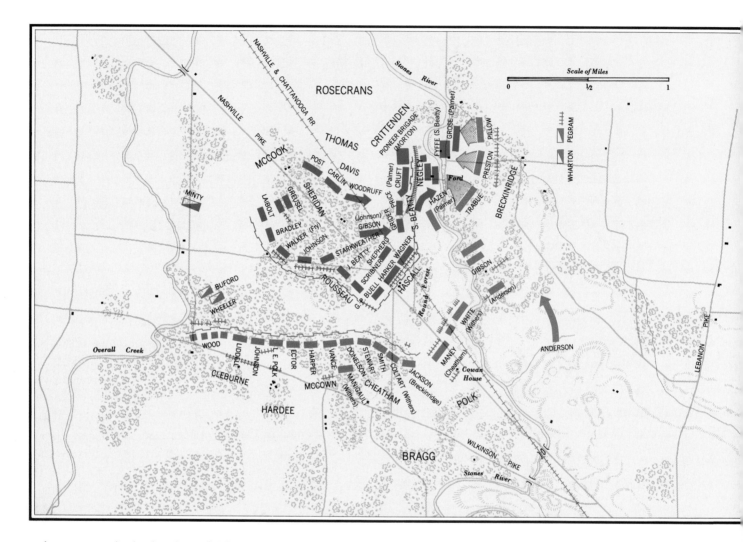

points to watch the battle unfold. Breckinridge took position behind the center of his second line; Bragg and Polk watched from Polk's headquarters near the Nashville Turnpike. Rosecrans, typically, was riding about inspecting his positions; at 4 p.m., he was at McFadden's Ford near Beatty's right flank. Rain and sleet had been falling all day. Now the infantrymen would have to fight in the miserable wet.

Beatty ordered the men on the exposed forward slope of the ridge to pull back behind the crest for protection from Confeder-

ate cannon fire. As the Federals scrambled rearward, precisely at 4 p.m., Breckinridge shouted, "Up, my men, and charge!" The order was repeated all along the half-mile length of the attack formation. And as soon as the Confederates stepped off, the guns of Beatty, and those of Mendenhall across the river, began to pour down a lethal rain of shells on the attackers.

Breckinridge reported afterward that he was proud of his soldiers' "admirable order" as they advanced at a quickstep across the 600 yards of open ground under the barrage. Ignoring their heavy casualties, the Confederates pressed forward, the first rank under orders to fire one volley and then use the bayonet.

When his front line was halfway to the ridge, Breckinridge noticed that the Federals overlapped his right flank. He ordered a halt while he brought up a battery of artillery and shifted units in the second line of infantry to extend his right. Then the Confederates resumed their march across the field and up the slope. As the distance between the opposing troops narrowed, an eerie silence fell; the gun crews ceased fire for fear of hitting their own men, and the infantrymen were holding their fire.

The ridge angled away from the Confederate line, and the Orphan Brigade on Breckinridge's left made contact first. Taking advantage of a protecting fold in the terrain, Hanson's men were able to advance under cover to within 150 yards of the Federal line. The moment they came into view, they drew a volley from Price's men — the 51st Ohio, 8th Kentucky and 35th Indiana — lying behind a rail fence. The Kentuckians let out what an Ohioan called "a most hideous yell," leveled a volley and charged with bayonets flashing. The Federals rose and fired again, but they could not stop the charge.

The Confederates on Breckinridge's right also were unstoppable. One of Pillow's regiments, the 20th Tennessee, rushed to a fence and leveled volley after volley at the Federals before them. "We had the advantage," recalled Private William J. McMurray, "and the slaughter was terrible." Sensing the opportunity, the Tennesseans resumed their charge. McMurray wrote: "The regiment did not take the time to climb the fence,

but caught it about the third rail from the bottom, and the fence, men and all went over together."

All along the line, Confederate troops stormed to the top of the crest. The brigades of Hanson and Pillow crashed into the ranks of Federal defenders, and savage hand-to-hand fighting commenced. On the Federal left, Colonel Bernard F. Mullen realized that his flanks were crumbling: "To prevent useless destruction of life, or entire capture of my regiment, I gave the order to retire. I was obliged to repeat it, and even then the brave fellows complied reluctantly — many refused, and they were either killed or captured."

The Federals on the ridge faltered and then gave way, moving rearward. As their flight became a rout, they overran Grider's reserve brigade behind them. Grider reported, "I allowed the retreating mass to pass through my lines, the enemy all the time pouring into us a destructive fire." Grider's Federals fought back fiercely, standing their ground. Colonel Grider rode up to Beatty and shouted, "We have them checked! Give us artillery and we will whip them!" But Grider's luck did not hold. At about this time, the 6th Kentucky, a regiment of Hanson's that had been pushed out of position in the Confederate charge, arrived unexpectedly on Grider's left flank and slammed into the 19th Ohio. The Ohioans gave way; Grider was flanked, and he gave the order to fall back and rally at the foot of the ridge.

The Confederates raced ahead in hot pursuit, sweeping Beatty's entire line before them. In less than 30 minutes, Breckinridge's division had achieved an objective thought impossible. It was time to stop, bring up the artillery and dig in on the ridge for the night. But the sight of the fleeing Federals was too much for the victorious Confederates. They had suffered for six days without hot food or proper shelter; they had slept and fought in the rain and sleet and freezing weather, and now they wanted nothing more than to get the battle over with and get their hands on the abundant supplies they hoped to find in the Federal camps. Disregarding their orders and the shouts of their officers, they chased the routed Federals all the way to the river. The 2nd and 6th Kentucky of Hanson's Orphan Brigade, leading the chase, actually crossed the river, expecting the rest of Breckinridge's men to follow.

But the Confederates were already paying dearly for their excess of zeal. The moment they crossed the crest of the ridge, they came into full view of Mendenhall's batteries across the river. At that point, Mendenhall's gunners went to work, and the ferocity of their cannonade, a Federal observer wrote, must have made it seem to the Confederates as though they had "opened the door of Hell, and the devil himself was there to greet them." Shells slammed into the pursuers at the rate of 100 rounds per minute, cutting great swaths from the Confederate ranks.

In Pillow's brigade, color-bearer George Lowe of the 18th Tennessee was cut down, and Private William McKay caught the falling banner. McKay himself was shot through the right thigh and dropped to the ground. Seeing this, the 18th's commander, Colonel Nat Gooch, shouted for a nearby soldier to take up the colors. "Pick it up yourself!" was the reply. Gooch did so, only to be shot through the shoulder. In all, six color-bearers of the 18th fell that day. General

Hanson, hit by a shell in the left knee, went down, mortally wounded. The pursuit slowed, and the disorganized survivors began milling about in desperate clusters in the river and on both banks. There, unable to endure the slaughter, they began to retreat back up the slope.

At that point, a Federal commander west of the river seized the initiative. Acting on his own authority, Colonel John F. Miller ordered his brigade to attack. While Rosecrans and Crittenden watched approvingly from the crest of a nearby hill, Miller's brigade charged across the river and slammed into the disorganized remnants of Hanson's and Pillow's brigades. Miller's men were soon followed by regiments from Stanley's brigade, which was ordered forward by Rosecrans, and then by units from Negley's and Palmer's divisions. The tide of battle was now reversed.

The Confederate officers tried desperately to halt the retreat on the crest of the hill they had just won. Colonel Joseph Lewis struggled to regroup his 6th Kentucky and the 2nd Kentucky, shouting to the men above the roar of Federal cannon to rally around their colors. But every time a color-bearer raised the flag, he was shot down. In a few minutes, the two regiments lost four color-bearers, while another regiment, the 4th Kentucky, lost three. In the absence of Hanson, Colonel R. P. Trabue took command of the Orphan Brigade and managed to stem the general retreat momentarily on the crest of the ridge, but try as he might, Trabue failed to rally the men.

When the Federal counterattackers had driven to within 150 yards of the top of the ridge, Miller ordered the 78th Pennsylvania to capture a Confederate battery posted

on the crest. As the Pennsylvanians rushed forward, they were joined by the rest of the brigade. Miller's men swarmed over the Confederate gunners, killing some and driving away the rest. Jimmy Thorne, a 16-year-old Pennsylvanian, climbed up on the barrel of a Confederate gun, patted it and yelled, "Here it is."

By 4:45 p.m., the rout of the Confederates was complete. On Bragg's orders, Brigadier General J. Patton Anderson's brigade moved across the river to help cover Breckinridge's retreat to his original lines. By then it was almost dark, and the Federals were willing to call it quits for the day.

Breckinridge was shattered by the pointless carnage. He watched numbly as his decimated and demoralized troops re-formed their ranks. When he saw how much shorter the lines were, he turned livid with anger at Bragg. A Kentucky officer reported that Breckinridge "was raging like a wounded lion as he passed the different commands from right to left. Tears broke from his eyes when he beheld the little remnants of his own old brigade." Then Breckinridge cried out, "My poor Orphans! My poor Orphans! My poor Orphan Brigade! They have cut it to pieces."

The rain and sleet, which had stopped at dusk, resumed as darkness engulfed the battlefield. Then began the usual ghastly task of clearing away the dead and trying to help the wounded. The meager medical facilities of both sides were swamped, especially the Confederate hospitals in Murfreesboro.

War-hardened men, Federal and Confederate, were shocked by the casualties, and they showed it in many ways, from tearful grief to sullen silence. General Rosecrans gave a local minister permission to take the body of Confederate Brigadier General James E. Rains to Nashville for burial at home. But he recoiled at the thought that Confederates in Nashville might use the funeral as an excuse for a rally. Rosecrans told the minister grimly: "I wish it to be distinctly understood that there is to be no

In the handwriting across the top of the sketch:

Make the trees as full of branches as you c... n, sky clear
the timber is very thick

Rebels charging thro... sh their men in close column

64 oh etc

Sundry corn

98 oh—
78

Charge assaults
Rebels in column forms
under the opposite banks
battle line

Flat limestone Rocks
everywhere jutting from
the ground.

View of
Lime Rock

In a sketch looking southward down Stones River, Ohio and Illinois troops ford the rapidly flowing stream and form up along the east bank. At left, Confe

The Battle of Stone River —
The decisive charge across Stone River Friday aft——
4° cl—

— River clear and
rapid —

fuss made over this affair. I will not permit it, sir, in the face of this bleeding army. My own officers are here, dead and unburied, and the bodies of my brave soldiers are yet on the field. You may have the corpse, sir; but remember distinctly that you cannot have an infernal secession 'pow-wow' over it in Nashville."

Rosecrans prepared for still more fighting. He ordered his troops to build defenses, and was much relieved when Brigadier General James G. Spears arrived from Nashville in the early-morning hours leading his brigade and a train of 303 wagons crammed with ammunition and hospital supplies. More help came later; Colonel Dan McCook arrived with a brigade of Tennesseans.

On his left flank, Rosecrans staged yet another of his deceptions to encourage Bragg to overestimate the Federal strength. Assembling three stentorian-voiced officers and a group of soldiers, he set out with them to simulate massive troop movements in the fields east of the recaptured ridge. The general and his party spread out, bawling commands and lighting fires as they went, until they covered a front three quarters of a mile long. At about 9 p.m., Rosecrans returned to his headquarters, dirty, tired and caked with mud. But he cheerfully exclaimed over and over again, "Things is workin'. Things is workin'."

In the meantime, General Bragg ordered Hardee's corps — McCown's and Cleburne's divisions — to cross the river and move to the right flank to reinforce Breckinridge. At 10 p.m., Bragg held a meeting of his corps and division commanders to discuss their next move and in particular to ponder the disposition of Polk's divisions under Withers and Cheatham. Only those Confed-

nition wagons scramble to withdraw, and an officer prepares to shoot his wounded horse.

erates remained west of the river, and they were in danger of being cut off. The river, swollen from the rain that continued to fall, would soon be too high to ford. The generals could not agree on the best course of action, so they decided to adjourn. General Bragg went to bed.

A little past midnight, Bragg was awakened by a courier with a report that the Federals were threatening on the right flank — the fruit of Rosecrans' clever decep-

tion. Another discouraging message arrived: At 2 a.m., General Polk passed along to Bragg a note he had received from Cheatham and Withers, who were becoming extremely nervous about their situation. Withers had suffered 33 per cent casualties, and Cheatham 15 per cent. Between them, they now commanded only 7,000 men able to fight. Rosecrans, they wrote, still had the bulk of his army opposite their lines. They warned that Stones River would become un-

desperate hilltop melee, Feder-
ops of the 78th Pennsylvania
whelm a Confederate battery
apture the battle flag of the
Tennessee (mistakenly identi-
s the 25th Tennessee in this
emporary lithograph).

fordable very soon, making their withdrawal extremely difficult. And they advised Bragg to retreat: "We do fear great disaster from the condition of things now existing, and think it should be averted if possible."

In forwarding the note, General Polk added a message of his own: "I very greatly fear the consequences of another engagement at this place. We could now, perhaps, get off with some safety and some credit, if the affair is well managed." Bragg barely glanced at the notes. Then he told Polk's courier, "Say to the general we shall maintain our position at every hazard."

Polk sent Hardee copies of all the notes, including Bragg's reply. Polk also wrote Hardee that he thought Bragg's decision was "unwise, in a high degree."

Nothing had changed by dawn on January 3. The armies were more or less in the same positions; the weather was still miserable; the river continued to rise; the wounded continued to suffer and die. But General Bragg began to see things in a different light. During the night, he had received word from Wheeler's cavalry of the arrival of Spears's brigade to reinforce Rosecrans. Bragg had also read documents captured during the attack on December 31. The information convinced him that Rosecrans now had an overwhelming numerical advantage — 70,000 men to face the 20,000 Confederates still able to fight. Bragg now conceded that Withers and Cheatham could soon be isolated on the left. He even admitted that his army was beginning to come apart after five days of exposure to the elements and enemy fire, with little rest and poor rations.

At 10 a.m., Bragg called in Hardee and Polk for a conference. The two corps com-

manders were quick to agree with Bragg's sudden assertion that retreat was necessary. As if it had been obvious all along, Bragg later declared, "Common prudence and the safety of my army, upon which the safety of our cause depended, left no doubt in my mind as to the necessity of my withdrawal from so unequal a contest."

It was finally over. During the afternoon of the 3rd, Bragg began sending his ammunition and supply wagons south toward Shelbyville and Manchester. Polk was ordered to take his troops out during the evening and move to Shelbyville. Hardee was to follow in the morning and march to Tullahoma. Behind him, Bragg left 1,700 seriously wounded and sick scattered among the homes of Murfreesboro.

The struggle along Stones River had cost the Confederates desperately. Of the 34,732 troops Bragg commanded when the battle began, he lost 9,239 killed or wounded — 27 per cent of his strength. Rosecrans lost 9,532 killed and wounded, 23 per cent of the 41,400 Federals engaged. But Bragg's losses were far more serious than the statistics indicated: The Federals could easily replace their casualties, but the thinly populated Confederacy was growing increasingly short of fighting men.

Although Rosecrans was astonished by Bragg's withdrawal, it did not take him long to realize that the outcome represented a major victory for the North. It made Kentucky safe for the Union and secured Nashville as a base for future Federal operations. It boosted the spirits of pro-Union East Tennesseans and dashed the hopes of Confederate sympathizers in central Tennessee and Kentucky. Moreover, for the Lincoln Administration the triumph was a much-needed antidote to

the recent Federal defeats at Fredericksburg and at Chickasaw Bayou, near Vicksburg. The President was elated. "God bless you," he telegraphed Rosecrans.

Bragg's retreat after his declaration of victory spread dismay throughout the Confederacy. Newspapers and the public renewed their angry cries for Bragg's head. The Chattanooga *Daily Rebel*, along with other newspapers, declared that Bragg had lost the confidence of his generals. Furthermore, various newspapers, including the *Rebel*, charged that he had retreated from Stones River against his generals' advice.

This allegation was untrue, and Bragg, outraged, decided to make an issue of it. "It becomes necessary for me to save my fair name," he declared in a letter to his corps and division commanders. He wanted them, he said, to help him end the "deluge of abuse" that was raining down on him.

"Unanimous as you were in council in verbally advising a retrograde movement, I cannot doubt that you will cheerfully attest the same in writing. I desire that you will consult your subordinate commanders and be candid with me."

The gambit might have worked to Bragg's satisfaction had he not added a fateful sentence: "I shall retire without a regret if I find I have lost the good opinion of my generals, upon whom I have ever relied as upon a foundation of rock."

Bragg had built his foundation on sand. All five of the generals who received Bragg's letter absolved him of the newspaper charge that he had retreated against their advice, and all five of them declared that he did not have their confidence. General Hardee's response was typical, offering all of the candor that Bragg had requested and a good deal more than he wanted: "Frankness compels me to say that the general officers whose judgment you have invoked are unanimous in their opinion that a change in the command of this army is necessary. In this opinion I concur."

Jefferson Davis was appalled at this new outburst of acrimony in the troublesome west. "Why General Bragg should have selected that tribunal and have invited its judgments upon him is to me unexplained," Davis wrote in an exasperated letter to General Joseph E. Johnston, the man he had placed in overall command in the vain hope of ending this kind of bickering. "It manifests, however, a condition of things which seems to me to require your presence. Although my confidence in General Bragg is unshaken, it cannot be doubted that if he is distrusted by his officers and troops, a disaster may result."

Johnston, awash in troubles, distracted and suffering from the wounds he had received the previous June, was on an inspection trip to Mobile, Alabama, when Davis' letter reached him. After having disagreed bitterly with Davis over strategy in the west, Johnston had predicted that the movements Davis had forced him to make would result in defeat both at Vicksburg and in East Tennessee. Now Johnston could take little satisfaction from seeing his predictions coming true.

Reluctantly, Johnston went to Bragg's headquarters at Tullahoma and for more than a week conducted an investigation of conditions there. By that time, Bragg was doing what he did best — managing a resting army — and Johnston reported to Richmond that whatever the complaints of Bragg's subordinates, the troops were in good shape and there was no reason to replace the commander.

But on returning to Mobile, Johnston received instructions from Confederate Secretary of War James A. Seddon to go back to Tullahoma, order Bragg to Richmond and take personal command of the Army of Tennessee. Once again, however, a seemingly clear-cut course of action soon became muddled. Arriving in Tullahoma, Johnston found Bragg distraught by the illness of his wife, who was believed to be dying. Johnston considerately delayed the execution of his orders, but then found his own health failing; by the time Bragg was able to return to duty, Johnston wrote later, "I was unfit for it." Declaring himself unable to serve in the field, Johnston went off to recover and left Bragg in command by default.

In the weeks after the battle at Stones River, Bragg managed — as usual — to avoid unpleasant realities. He rejected responsibility for his defeat and placed the blame on his commanders, especially Cheatham, Breckinridge, Polk and Hardee. He did not see that his sour, suspicious nature had infected an army that had fought well and deserved better.

Bragg simply turned his back on Murfreesboro and went on with drilling and training his men. In his eyes, the battle just delayed the opportunity to deal the enemy a crippling blow. He knew that Rosecrans would have to take Chattanooga in order to control Tennessee and invade Georgia from the west. And when the Federals moved against Chattanooga, Bragg and the Army of Tennessee would be waiting for them along the banks of the Chickamauga.

105th Ohio, part of Rosecrans' of the Cumberland, marches Murfreesboro after the battle. gh the fighting left the town uned, almost every building had turned into a hospital for the ded and dying of both sides. e often expressed the desire ness the terrible strife of a battle," wrote an Illinois soldier tter home, "but I can say now ny curiosity is fully satisfied."

General Breckinridge's Confederates *(background, right)* attack the Federal line near Hell's Half Acre during the first day at Stones River. Massed fire from the a

Battlescapes from an Infantryman

he most compelling record of the bat-
at Stones River is to be found not
the memoirs of high-ranking offi-
rs but in a series of pictures by an
scure Federal infantryman and self-
ight artist, Private Alfred E. Math-
s. Mathews saw the fighting at first
nd, enduring the cold, hunger and
ror of the three-day standoff. The
hographs shown here and on the fol-
wing pages, made from his battlefield
awings, evoke the violent ebb and flow
the combat as he and his comrades
perienced it.

Mathews was well equipped to make

such a visual record. Coming from an
artistically inclined family of English im-
migrants that had settled in Ohio, he was
an enthusiastic landscapist. When the
Civil War broke out, he was teaching
school in Alabama; he fled the South and
soon enlisted in the Union Army, ending
up in the 31st Ohio Volunteers. His regiment saw action at Shiloh and several
subsequent battles, and by the time he
got to Stones River, Mathews was a sea-
soned veteran. He was also an experienced military topographer. His commanders, recognizing his artistic ability,
had set him to drawing battlefield maps.

Mathews' military experience and
graphic skills came together in his pictures of Stones River. These works faith-
fully depict the terrain and render the
armies' actual movements with surpris-
ing accuracy. They are also enriched by
Mathews' eye for the revealing detail.
During the fighting on December 31,
retreating Federal troops abandoned a
row of overcoats on the field. Advancing Confederates, mistaking the coats
for prone infantrymen, peppered them
with musket fire. The coats appear,
suitably tattered, on the right of the
lithograph below.

fantry of General Lovell Rousseau's division (*foreground*), wedged between the Nashville Pike and the railroad, beat off the assault, inflicting heavy losses.

Reinforcing the crumbling Federal right flank, Ohio, Indiana and Kentucky troops of General Samuel Beatty's brigade *(foreground)* stagger General Cleb

king Confederates with a sharp volley around noon on the first day of battle. Nevertheless, Beatty was soon forced to retire as units to his right and left fell back.

On the third day of the battle, January 2, 1863, the 2,200 men of Colonel John Miller's Federal brigade ford the shallow Stones River, pursuing General Breckin

ederates (*background*) after the failure of their assault. Miller's spirited counterattack, undertaken on his own initiative, was halted only by darkness.

At 4 p.m. on January 2, Colonel Moses Walker's Federal brigade — with artist Mathews' own 31st Ohio in the front line on the left — counterattacks the Confedera

men formed their lines, and moved to the front with a veteran steadiness and determination," Walker said. Under the fierce attack, the Confederates withdrew.

In another action on January 2, a Federal division led by General Rousseau, seen riding between his lines ahead of an aide (center), engages General Polk's Confed

from the distant treeline. In the foreground, the men of the 21st Wisconsin, stationed in reserve, lie prone to avoid the Confederate shellfire.

ACKNOWLEDGMENTS

The editors thank the following individuals and institutions for their valuable assistance in the preparation of this volume: *Kentucky:* Danville — Kurt Holman; Frankfort — Nicky Hughes, Kentucky Military History Museum. Lexington — Bettie L. Kerr, The Lexington Fayette County Historic Commission.
Maryland: Adamstown — Denis E. Reen.
Nebraska: Omaha — Dr. Lon W. Keim.
Ohio: Columbus — Tauni Graham, Ohio Historical Society.
Oklahoma: Fort Sill — Towana D. Spivey, Fort Sill Museum.
Pennsylvania: Carlisle — Randy Hackenburg, Michael J. Winey, U.S. Army Military History Institute.
Tennessee: Chattanooga — Jill Avel, Chattanooga Museum of Regional History. Nashville — James Hoobler, Tennessee Historical Society; James C. Kelly, Shelley Reisman Paine, Dan E. Pomeroy, Tennessee State Museum. Gallatin — Walter Durham.
Virginia: Alexandria — Susan Cumby, Wanda Dowell, Walton Owen, Fort Ward Museum. Falls Church — Chris Nelson. Manassas — Michael Andrus, Roland R. Swain, nassas National Battlefield Park; Richard Catter, Eagle I Arsenal. Richmond — David Hahn, Museum of Confederacy.
Washington, D.C.: Eveline Nave, Photoduplication vice, Library of Congress; Dan Stanton, National Museu American History, Smithsonian Institution.
Wisconsin: Madison — Lynette Wolfe, G.A.R. Museu

The index for this book was prepared by Roy Nanovic.

LIOGRAPHY

ks

y, John, *The Citizen-Soldier: or, Memoirs of a Volunteer.* llector's Library of the Civil War. Alexandria, Va.: ne-Life Books (reprint of 1879 edition).

kburn, Theodore W., *Letters From the Front: A Union reacher" Regiment (74th Ohio) in the Civil War.* Dayton: orningside Bookshop, 1981.

in, B. A., ed., *A Civil War Treasury of Tales, Legends and lklore.* New York: Promontory Press, 1981.

, Irving A., *Cleburne and His Command.* Dayton: Mornside Bookshop, 1982.

, G. Craig, *Historic Southern Saddles 1840-1865.* Enola, .: Civil War Antiquities, 1982.

n, Bruce, *This Hallowed Ground: The Story of the Union de of the Civil War.* New York: Pocket Books, Inc., 1961.

nut, Mary Boykin, *Mary Chesnut's Civil War.* Ed. by C. nn Woodward. New Haven: Yale University Press, 81.

War Centennial Commission, *Tennesseans in the Civil ar: A Military History of Confederate and Union Units with ailable Rosters of Personnel,* Part 1. Nashville: Civil War ntennial Commission, 1964.

ves, Freeman, *Rock of Chickamauga: The Life of General orge H. Thomas.* Norman: University of Oklahoma ess, 1948.

ins, Jack, *Arms and Equipment of the Civil War.* Garden ty, N.Y.: Doubleday & Company, Inc., 1962.

nelly, Thomas Lawrence, *my of the Heartland: The Army of Tennessee, 1861-1862.* ton Rouge: Louisiana State University Press, 1967. utumn of Glory: The Army of Tennessee, 1862-1865.* Baton ouge: Louisiana State University Press, 1971.

nelly, Thomas Lawrence, and Archer Jones, *The Politics Command: Factions and Ideas in Confederate Strategy.* Ba n Rouge: Louisiana State University Press, 1973.

nolly, James A., *Three Years in the Army of the Cumber nd: The Letters and Diary of Major James A. Connolly.* Ed. Paul M. Angle. Bloomington: Indiana University Press, 59.

iel, Larry J., *Cannoneers in Gray: The Field Artillery of the my of Tennessee, 1861-1865.* University: The University Alabama Press, 1984.

ey, Thomas S., and Peter C. George, *Field Artillery Pro tiles of the American Civil War.* Ed. by Floyd W. McRae . Atlanta: Arsenal Press, 1980.

e, Basil W.: *History of Morgan's Cavalry.* Ed. by Cecil Fletcher Hol nd. Bloomington: Indiana University Press, 1960. organ's Cavalry.* New York: The Neale Publishing Com ny, 1906. eminiscences of General Basil W. Duke, C.S.A.* Freeport, .Y.: Books for Libraries Press, 1969 (reprint of 1911 ition).

, John P., *"Fightin' Joe" Wheeler.* University: Louisiana ate University Press, 1941.

ards, William B., *Civil War Guns: The Complete Story of deral and Confederate Small Arms.* New York: Castle ooks, 1962.

osito, Vincent J., ed., *The West Point Atlas of American ars,* Vol. 1. New York: Frederick A. Praeger, 1959.

h, John, *Annals of the Army of the Cumberland.* Philadel hia: J. B. Lippincott & Co., 1864.

e, Shelby: he Civil War, A Narrative: Fort Sumter to Perryville.* New

York: Random House, 1958. *The Civil War, A Narrative: Fredericksburg to Meridian.* New York: Random House, 1963.

Fox, William F., *Regimental Losses in The American Civil War 1861-1865.* Albany, N.Y.: Albany Publishing Company, 1893.

Garesché, Louis, *Biography of Lieut. Col. Julius P. Garesché.* Philadelphia: J. B. Lippincott Company, 1887.

Garfield, James A., *The Wild Life of the Army: Civil War Letters of James A. Garfield.* Ed. by Frederick D. Williams. East Lansing: Michigan State University Press, 1964.

Gibbon, John, *The Artillerist's Manual.* Westport, Conn.: Greenwood Press, Publishers, 1971 (reprint of 1860 edition).

Green, Johnny, *Johnny Green of the Orphan Brigade: The Jour nal of a Confederate Soldier.* Ed. by A. D. Kirwan. Lexing ton: The University of Kentucky Press, 1956.

Hafendorfer, Kenneth A., *Perryville: Battle for Kentucky.* Owensboro, Ky.: McDowell Publications, 1981.

Hazlett, James C., Edwin Olmstead and M. Hume Parks, *Field Artillery Weapons of the Civil War.* Newark: Universi ty of Delaware Press, 1983.

Horn, Stanley F., *The Army of Tennessee.* Norman: University of Oklahoma Press, 1941.

Horn, Stanley F., comp. and ed., *Tennessee's War 1861-1865: Described by Participants.* Nashville: Tennessee Civil War Centennial Commission, 1965.

Johnson, Robert Underwood, and Clarence Clough Buel, eds.: *Battles and Leaders of the Civil War,* Vol. 3. New York: The Century Co., 1887. *Battles and Leaders of the Civil War: North to Antietam.* New York: Castle Books, 1956.

Jones, J. B., *A Rebel War Clerk's Diary at the Confederate States Capital,* Vol. 1. Ed. by Howard Swiggett. New York: Old Hickory Bookshop, 1935.

Jordan, Thomas, and J. P. Pryor, *The Campaigns of Lieut.- Gen. N. B. Forrest, and of Forrest's Cavalry.* New York: Blelock & Company, 1868.

Lamers, William M., *The Edge of Glory: A Biography of Gen eral William S. Rosecrans, U.S.A.* New York: Harcourt, Brace & World, Inc., 1961.

Lytle, Andrew Nelson, *Bedford Forrest and His Critter Com pany.* New York: G. P. Putnam's Sons, 1931.

McDonough, James Lee, *Stones River: Bloody Winter in Ten nessee.* Knoxville: The University of Tennessee Press, 1980.

McWhiney, Grady, *Braxton Bragg and Confederate Defeat,* Vol. 1. New York: Columbia University Press, 1969.

Madaus, Howard Michael, *The Battle Flags of the Confederate Army of Tennessee.* Milwaukee: Milwaukee Public Muse um, 1976.

Owen, Wm. Miller, *In Camp and Battle with the Washington Artillery of New Orleans.* Boston: Ticknor and Company, 1885.

Peterson, Harold L., *Round Shot and Rammers.* New York: Bonanza Books, 1969.

Pittenger, William, *Daring and Suffering: A History of the Great Railroad Adventure.* Collector's Library of the Civil War. Alexandria, Va.: Time-Life Books (reprint of 1863 edition).

Polk, William M., *Leonidas Polk: Bishop and General,* Vols. 1 and 2. New York: Longmans, Green, and Co., 1915.

Ripley, Warren, *Artillery and Ammunition of the Civil War.* New York: Promontory Press, 1970.

Roberts, Joseph, *The Hand-Book of Artillery, for the Service of the United States.* New York: D. Van Nostrand, 1860.

Sheridan, P. H., *Personal Memoirs of P. H. Sheridan,* Vol. 1. St. Clair Shores, Mich.: Scholarly Press, Inc., 1977 (reprint of 1888 edition).

Smith, Page, *Trial by Fire,* Vol. 5. New York: McGraw-Hill Book Company, 1982.

Strode, Hudson, *Jefferson Davis: Confederate President.* New York: Harcourt, Brace and Company, 1959.

Swiggett, Howard, *The Rebel Raider: A Life of John Hunt Morgan.* Indianapolis: Bobbs-Merrill Company, 1934.

Todd, Frederick P., *American Military Equipage 1851-1872.* New York: Charles Scribner's Sons, 1980.

Tucker, Glenn, *Chickamauga: Bloody Battle in the West.* Day ton: Morningside Bookshop, 1976.

United States War Department, *The War of the Rebellion: A Compilation of the Official Records of the Union and Confeder ate Armies,* Series 1: Vol. 16, Part I — Reports, Part II — Correspondence; Vol. 17, Part II — Correspondence; and Vol. 20, Part I — Reports, Part II — Correspondence Wash ington: Government Printing Office, 1886-1887.

Van Horne, Thomas B.: *History of the Army of the Cumberland: Its Organization, Campaigns, and Battles,* Vol. 1. Cincinnati: Robert Clarke & Co., 1875. *The Life of Major-General George H. Thomas.* New York: Charles Scribner's Sons, 1882.

Warner, Ezra J.: *Generals in Blue: Lives of the Union Commanders.* Baton Rouge: Louisiana State University Press, 1964. *Generals in Gray: Lives of the Confederate Commanders.* Ba ton Rouge: Louisiana State University Press, 1959.

Watkins, Sam R., *"Co. Aytch": A Side Show of the Big Show.* New York: Collier Books, 1962.

Wiley, Bell Irvin: *The Life of Billy Yank: The Common Soldier of the Union.* Baton Rouge: Louisiana State University Press, 1981. *The Life of Johnny Reb: The Common Soldier of the Confeder acy.* New York: Bobbs-Merrill Company, 1943.

Williams, Kenneth P.: *Lincoln Finds a General: Grant's First Year in the West,* Vol. 3. New York: The MacMillan Company, 1952. *Lincoln Finds a General: Iuka to Vicksburg,* Vol. 4. New York: The MacMillan Company, 1956.

Wyeth, John Allan, *Life of General Nathan Bedford Forrest.* Dayton: Morningside Bookshop, 1975.

Yater, George H., *Two Hundred Years at the Falls of the Ohio: A History of Louisville and Jefferson County.* Louisville, Ky.: The Heritage Corporation of Louisville and Jefferson County, 1979.

Other Sources

Bryan, Charles F., Jr., " 'I Mean To Have Them All': For rest's Murfreesboro Raid." *Civil War Times Illustrated,* Jan uary 1974.

Horn, Stanley F., "The Battle of Stones River." *Civil War Times Illustrated* Special Edition, 1983.

McWhiney, Grady, "Controversy in Kentucky: Braxton Bragg's Campaign of 1862." *Civil War History,* March 1960.

Morsberger, Robert E., "The Savior of Cincinnati." *Civil War Times,* November 1972.

Walker, Hugh, "Spy Preserved Civil War Letters." *The Ten nessean,* August 5, 1979.

INDEX